Love
CONSCIOUSNESS

Love
CONSCIOUSNESS

BRIAN TOLIVER

authorHOUSE®

AuthorHouse™ LLC
1663 Liberty Drive
Bloomington, IN 47403
www.authorhouse.com
Phone: 1-800-839-8640

Published by AuthorHouse   04/29/2014

ISBN: 978-1-4969-0960-2 (sc)
ISBN: 978-1-4969-0958-9 (hc)
ISBN: 978-1-4969-0959-6 (e)

Library of Congress Control Number: 2014907988

This book is printed on acid-free paper.

Because of the dynamic nature of the Internet, any web addresses or links contained in this book may have changed since publication and may no longer be valid. The views expressed in this work are solely those of the author and do not necessarily reflect the views of the publisher, and the publisher hereby disclaims any responsibility for them.

Scripture quotations marked AMP are from The Amplified Bible, Old Testament copyright © 1965, 1987 by the Zondervan Corporation. The Amplified Bible, New Testament copyright © 1954, 1958, 1987 by The Lockman Foundation. Used by permission. All rights reserved.

Scripture quotations marked KJV are from the Holy Bible, King James Version (Authorized Version). First published in 1611. Quoted from the KJV Classic Reference Bible, Copyright © 1983 by The Zondervan Corporation.

Scripture quotations marked NKJV are taken from the New King James Version. Copyright © 1982 by Thomas Nelson, Inc. Used by permission. All rights reserved.

CONTENTS

DEDICATION

To my mother, Gloria Toliver who showed me what love really means. To my family, my wife Doresa, my son Yashar, my daughters Kristen and Danielle, I love you more than you will ever know. To my first Granddaughter, Kalynn, I never knew the Love I have for you could be so great.

In memory to my Father, Josh Toliver who I miss so much. Thank you. You made me the man that I am.
In memory of my Friend Johnnie Dixon, we shared so much; God gave us a relationship that cannot be replaced. I miss you brother.

INTRODUCTION

There is a consciousness of the soul that God desires the believer to lay hold. This consciousness is the soul of the God. We are to think as God thinks. What moves God should move us. We are to express as God expresses His thoughts and feelings. This is the life of God that is given to the believer.

This book's inspiration came from my experiences with God and the message that He gave to me. God birthed in me this message in the streets of different cities. God has given to me Love and understanding. That Love and understanding has changed the lives of many people. Many of which did not believe in God. Receive the words written in this book and your life will change too! This is what I believe. Once you see God, as he is.

His Love will affect you in some way. The message reveals the intimacy of God and the content in God's soul. God's soul is His character and nature, His substance, His Life.

Yes, God has a soul. Many believers do not know this and God refers to His soul many times. In Leviticus 26:11-12 God (Elohiym) said *"And I will set my tabernacle among you: and my SOUL shall not abhor you. And I will walk among you, and will be your God, and ye shall be my people."* Also, in Matthew 12:18 God (The Father) speaking of Jesus "*Behold my servant, whom I have chosen my beloved, in whom my* SOUL *is well pleased: I will put my spirit upon him, and he shall show judgment to the Gentiles."* God's soul is what God is: "Love." The soul of man God created in the image of His soul. Therefore, man's soul God created in the image of LOVE. God said in Hebrews 10:16 (KJV)

"This is the covenant that I will make with them after those days, saith the Lord, I will put my laws into their hearts, and in their minds will I write them." God has written the laws of love on our hearts and minds. When the believer has this consciousness, he is full with all the fullness of God. The believer becomes a powerful worker of mighty works. He becomes an overcomer of the World. He becomes as the Father is.

How nature moans for the believer to come to a place of love consciousness. When the whole Body of Christ manifests this love consciousness, it will put our last enemy (death) under our feet. As He is so are we in this world, love is the victory!

CHAPTER I

BORN OF LOVE

I have often heard it proclaimed that the body of Christ needs to demonstrate love. Also, Christians should learn how to walk in love with one another. Over the years in ministry, I have seen various believers try to learn to walk in love toward each other unsuccessfully. These believers were from different religious backgrounds. None of whom realized love is not a learned behavior, but in Christ, love is a choice.

A mother does not learn how to love her child. She desired a child and acted on her desire. The actions of her desire produced a child. Her desire to have a child is her choice to love her child. Mothers that did not desire a child or had their child due to situations out of her control love their child. A mother must choose not to love her child.

Therefore, a mother's love for her child is a choice. It is the same with the believer.

When the believer's desire to love becomes his choice, he will act on it. Your desire to love must be strong enough for you to act on.

Acting on your decision to love will produce love. This happens when the believer realizes he is born of God to love.

While attending Howard University, my first year, I stayed at my uncle's home. My aunt was a member of a Holiness Church. She was very strict concerning religious matters and practices in the house. It was a big adjustment for me coming into that type of environment. Even with all the rules I was under subjection, I thought it was wonderful to get to know my aunt, uncle, and cousins. One of my cousin, Tara and I became very close. She was very strong in academics and showed excitement about doing well in school. She wanted recognition for her academic achievements at home. I encouraged her to keep doing her best in school. She had looked up to me because I went from a sophomore to a senior. I had graduated from High School in three years. She did not know how much she influenced me. She had such a sweet spirit. I saw her supernatural capacity to give and receive love. She was my first example of someone born of Love (God). She consistently showed the love of God. God will show all. God will show that any person who lives a life of love is His child.

One day, I was sitting in the kitchen speaking with my aunt. I heard the sound of someone falling down the stairs. I jumped up out of my seat and ran to the stairs. When I arrived at the stairs, my cousin Tara was falling down the stairs. I caught her before she hit her head on the base of the stairs. My aunt arrived shortly afterwards. My aunt said to me; "Why did you jump up and run when you did?" I answered: "I ran because I heard her falling down the stairs." My aunt replied; "she did not hear her fall until after I got up and ran." Then I realized God had me hear her fall before she actually fell. It was not possible for me to arrive and catch her after hearing her fall. Especially, realizing where I was sitting and distance to the stairs. For me to catch her, I had to be on my way to the stairs before she started to fall. This realization was alarming. Why, would God use someone, who at the time was not a believer? Why would God use me to save someone from serious harm? God did this because the person in danger was special. God chose to show all present that she was his child.

1 John 4:7 (KJV) says *"Beloved, let us love one another for love is of God, and everyone that loveth is born of God, and knoweth God."* John is speaking to the believer, "Beloved, let us love one another". The word "let" indicates ability, choice, and action. Through John, the Holy Spirit is saying, you can love if you choose. If you choose, you will love. Why will you love? **You will love because you are born of God**. **This is a fundamental truth and the foundation for all believers**.

How is it that so many fail in walking in love towards the body of Christ? They were trying to love out of responsibility and not desire. The desire that brings you to your choice to love, calls your heart to love's action. You do not have to try something you can do. You do it. As a believer, you don't have to try to walk in love, you can do it. You are born of God. That fact gives you more than the ability to love.

Love is a manifested product of the Spirit. It is the criteria in which to measure whether or not you are born of God. To be born of God is to be born of the Spirit. Jesus said in John 3:6 "That which is born of the flesh is flesh and that which is born of the Spirit is spirit." Love is a spirit. God is love (1 John 4:8). If God is Spirit and He is love, then love is also a spirit. If you are Born Again, you are born of the spirit. If you are Born Again, you are born of God. Tying all these truths together brings you the revelation that you are BORN OF LOVE!

As love is God's substance, it is also our substance. You are born of His substance.

You are of His flesh and of His bones (Eph. 5:30). If you grasp that, you are born of His substance. You would see that you are a new creature (creation). We are of the species of Christ. We are a species with the substance of God and flesh.

God's ability would become a reality to you if you would take hold of what you are born. To grasp, choose, and be love is to know God. The word "know" in 1 John 4:7 in the Greek (Ginosko) means absolute knowledge. Absolute knowledge is total and complete knowledge. When we are love to one another, we absolutely know God.

Your spirit already knows God. Your spirit is the part of you that was Born Again.

There is a part of your soul that is spiritual and a part that is fleshly. Your soul dwells in your brain. There are two Greek words used in the scriptures for soul "Psuche" and "Pneuma." The word psuche means breath, spirit, heart, life, mind, soul. The word pneuma means a current of air, breath (blast) or a breeze a human spirit, the rational soul, life, mind, spirit. It also, is used in conjunction with an angel, demon, God, Christ's spirit, the Holy Spirit. Pneuma is never used in scriptures that refer to losing your soul, death of the soul, saving the soul and warring against your soul. Pneuma usually speaks of the whole spirit man when used in the context of the soul. Psuche is always used in the context of salvation, death and losing of one's soul.

Pneuma (soul) is that part of you that was Born Again. It is the real you. This part of your soul is the voice of your human spirit. It is the part God breathed into man and made your psuche (soul) alive. The psuche receives and gives messages to your spirit.

Whenever, we exercise our will we send a message to our spirit. It is the medium between our flesh and human spirit. That is it enables us to communicate and relate to the spiritual world and the natural world. When we set our will to love, the soul (psuche) will allow love to flow. It is the Love that we are born of and it will flow through our natural mind to others.

The knowledge of being born of love frees your soul to believe you are the Righteousness of God. Righteousness is the ability to stand before God without guilt, shame, inferiority, apprehension, or doubt. You will no longer doubt what God says you have and are in Him. Sin Consciousness becomes a part of the past.

"Perfect love casteth out fear" (1 John 4:18). "Fear" means to be regretfully inclined to think to be afraid to be in doubt apprehensive. Love casts out apprehension in approaching the Father. Love casts out anything you are regretfully inclined to think of (sin). Love casts out doubt in what the Father has declared you to be. Love delivers your soul (your feelings, emotions, intellect, will, and reasoning faculties).

For God so loved the world, that he gave his only begotten son that whosoever believeth (their soul) would not perish. God so loved, those who believe are born of love and this love delivers our soul from perishing or death.

One night while teaching a Bible study. I was explaining to the study group that they are born of love. That same love brings them to righteousness. Further, I taught that they did not have to hold on to the guilt and sin consciousness anymore. Then I demonstrated the love of God to them. I did this by putting my arms around them one at a time. Jesus did this with his disciples (John 13:23). I spoke the Father's heart (opinion, attitude and emotions) concerning them and each of them fell under the compassion or the power of Love. Love caused those that had not committed their life to God, to do so then.

Jesus promised that if you love Him, He and the Father would love you. He said they will manifest Themselves to you (John 14:21). Through the Holy Spirit, I introduced them to love. They received love, became love, and experienced the love of God.

They had no instructions on how to love one another. They began to love one another from that time on. The group would get together everyday and go over what they had learned. They would pray, edify, exhort, and manifest the love they experienced towards one another.

If you don't receive love, you cannot give love. Love is from the spirit and will influence your soul (your feelings, emotions, intellect, will, and reasoning faculties). I thank God for the Born Again experience. That experience is of Love, not fear. The experience of Love's substance effecting the will, emotions, feelings, intellect, and reasoning faculties.

God so loved, that He gave love to the world. We need to present the gospel in His love so the world can receive that love. The world needs the gospel presented free from fear, condemnation, guilt and indebtedness. Presenting the gospel, any other way is to change the spirit of the Word. Guilt, condemnation, fear, is not of God. The spirit of the Word is Love.

There is a spiritual law of sowing and reaping. ***"Whatever a man soweth, that shall he also reap"*** Galatians 6:7 (KJV). The heart is the ground where the seed is sown (Mark 4:15). The Word of God is the seed. Remember, the life (spirit) of the seed (Word) is love. A seed has enough life in it to produce of its own kind. If you sow seeds of condemnation, guilt, and fear, it will take root. The person's heart that gives ground to those seeds will produce fruit of condemnation, guilt and fear.

That is why so many fall away from the truth because they never received the love (seed) of the Father. Yes, there can be conviction without a transformation of the heart. This truth is evident in the life of Judas. Judas had conviction in his heart when he betrayed Jesus. Judas choose the transformation of death through suicide instead of the transformation of life through Love. When you sow the seed of love as Jesus did you will produce creations born of love. Love is the criteria of being born of God. Sowing love starts the believer on the path of living Love. *"By this shall men know ye are my disciples that ye have love one towards another."* John 13:35 (KJV).

Everything Jesus did was by example and precept. He demonstrated our new life. Jesus showed us the life of Love. You can exemplify the life of love because He said you could. Jesus would not tell you to do something that you could not. He showed love and the world recognized He was sent from the Father. When you demonstrate that, you are born of Love the world will see it. The world will recognize that you are of Jesus. The world will know that He sent you. By this shall men know who you are!

One with Love

Being born of love creates a new intimacy with the Father. This intimacy is greater than one between a husband and wife. It is an intimacy that surpasses all what we could ask or think possible.

Many believers say God is in them or with them but act as though he is a thousand miles away. There is an **attitude of ascension** that takes away the reality that God is in us. In Acts 1:11, the disciples were gazing up towards heaven after Jesus disappeared in a cloud. Many believers are in the mindset that Jesus left. That mindset makes it difficult to maintain a proper relationship with Jesus, because He is far away.

This attitude of ascension causes many to long for an intimacy they just cannot acquire. Frustration, insecurity, and depression breed from this attitude. No matter what is done. Regardless of the studying time made, or how long one prays, it never produces the intimacy desired.

God provides us with a oneness with Himself. All believers must come to the realization of our oneness with God. The believer's acceptance that he is beloved of God causes the realization. The revelation must come that the desired intimacy God established already. Jesus prayed in John 17:20-23

"And not in regard to these alone do I ask, but also in regard to those who shall be believing, through their word, in me; that they all may be one, as Thou Father art in me, and I in Thee; that they also in us may be one, that the world may believe that Thou didst send me. And I, the glory that thou hast given to me, have given to them, that they may be one as we are one; I in them, and Thou in me, that they may be perfected into one, and that the world may know that thou didst send me, and didst love them as Thou didst love me." (Young's Literal Translation)

Jesus' prayer covers all believers past, present, and future who believe through their word in Him. Jesus' request was that we be one as He and the Father are one. Jesus and the Father were one in spirit and soul. Jesus' body had nothing to do with this oneness. Jesus' flesh had to follow His will. Jesus' flesh had to come into obedience to His will. We see this in Philippians 2:5-8

"Let this mind be in you, which was also in Christ Jesus: Who, being in the form of God, thought it not robbery to be equal with God: But made himself of no reputation, and took upon him the form of a servant, and was made in the likeness of men: And being found in fashion as a man, he humbled Himself, and became obedient unto death, even the death of the cross."

Jesus' request was for us to be one as He and the Father are one. This request is for us to be one with Them in spirit and soul. The question is, would the Father grant His request or not? Jesus said that the Father always hears His request (John 11:42). If the Father did not grant His request, it would mean that He and the Father were not one.

Why would not granting Jesus' request mean the Father and Jesus were not one? This is because Jesus' prayer would not have been in line with the Father's will. Jesus said that

He does the Father will always (John 6:38). Therefore, anything else would mean that Jesus lied. The Father cannot be one with a lie. The Father granted His request. We are one with Jesus and the Father. Bless God. We don't have to labor for that oneness. We don't have to beg or plead for it. There is no need for us to sacrifice to have that oneness.

It comes through the believing of the Word. It comes through being born of **LOVE**.

There is nothing more intimate than the love that the Father shows Jesus. The relationship Jesus has with the Father is the closest relationship possible. We have this same relationship through love. The body of Christ will take hold of this relationship with God.

When this happens all believers will be on their way to perfection (John 17:23). *"And we have known and believed the love that God hath to us. God is love, and he that dwelleth in love dwelleth in God and God in Him."*1 John 4:16. It would be a more accurate translation of the beginning of that verse if it read, "*We have absolutely known and believed the love that God has in us.*" You should absolutely know the love that is in you, for you are born of it (1 John 4:7). You have become one with Love. Love dwells in you and you dwell in Love. Another way to say it is, that you live in Love and Love lives in you.

"If ye keep my commandments, ye shall abide in my love, even as I have kept my Father's commandments, and abide in his love (John 15:10)." If you keep His commandments, you will dwell in His Love the same way Jesus kept the Father's commandments and dwells in His Love.

We are Love as He is Love in this world

You are born of Love. You live in Love. Love lives in you and you know Love.

God is Love. *"As He is so are we in this world (1 John 4:17)."* You are all the Father is in this world. You are all that Jesus is in this world. No longer can we exclaim, "I want to be like Jesus." We are as He is.

There is a great difference in being like someone and being as that person is. Suppose, I was playing basketball and someone said to me, "You play like Michael Jordan." That would mean my actions are similar to his. Now, if they said to me, "You play as Michael Jordan plays." It would mean he and I play basketball exactly the same. There should be no difference in Jesus and us. The problem is that the body of Christ has not come to that realization. It is not enough for the world to see the body of Christ act like Jesus. We must walk as He walked. The problem is the world see's the body act like Jesus but not walking as Jesus walked. The call that we must walk as He walked is stated clearly in 1 John 2:5-6

"But whosoever keepeth His Word, in him verily is the love of God perfected by this know we that we are in Him. He that

saith he abideth in Him ought himself also so to walk, even as He walked."(KJV)

You know you abide in Him, but do you know you can walk even as He walked? In this verse, keeping His Word is synonymous with love (1 John 4:12). Jesus is the Word.

Jesus and the Father are one. The Father is Love. Jesus is Love. The Word is Love! Isn't that Good News? God so loved, that He sent Love (Jesus, the expressed image of God) so you can be born of Love. God so loved, that He sent Love, so you can know Love, and be one with Love.

The revelation that the Word is Love will open the door for many other revelations. As you are reading, studying, meditating, or speaking the Word, the Word will take on a new dimension in your soul. For the Word (Love) will come alive and abide in you. Then you will realize you are one with the Word, one with Love, even as the Father and the Son are one.

To get the impact of what God has declared, let us look at John 5:17-18.

"But Jesus answered them, My Father worketh hitherto, and I work. Therefore, the Jews sought the more to kill him, because he

not only had broken the Sabbath, but said also that God was his Father, making himself equal with God."

The Jews wanted to kill Jesus for saying God was His Father. The fact is God is our Father also. In John 10:30 Jesus said, *"I and my Father are one."* The Jews once again took up stones to stone him (John 10:31). The Jews understood what Jesus was saying.

John 10:33, the Jews answering Jesus' question said; *"For a Good work we stone thee not, but for blasphemy and because that thou, being a man, makest thyself God."* The Jews understood what Jesus said made Him God or equal with God. God has declared **WE ARE ONE WITH JESUS AND THE FATHER!** What does that statement mean to us? Are we making ourselves as God through our statement of being one with God and Jesus? As He is so are we in this world! I didn't say that God did. I know this statement will anger some people, but the truth causes this type of reaction in those who resist it.

All the Devil tried to make himself through sin, God gave to us through Love. Love gives us dominion over the work of His hands and over evil. Anything else wouldn't be to abide in Love.

Maybe now, you can begin to see how you are a new creation of Love. Can you see how Love makes righteousness a reality, and creates a new intimacy with the Father that is unsurpassable?

The intimacy that you have received from God is unsurpassable because God put Himself in you. There is nothing more intimate than another being inside your thoughts, feelings and body. Furthermore, He has sealed that intimacy with the Holy Spirit. It is through the Holy Spirit that He gives us His love and makes known unto us the life of Love. That Love life that the Holy Spirit reveals to us produces fruit in the believer's life. This fruit is fruit that the world can feast on and will produce Love in those that eat of it.

CHAPTER II

THE HOLY SPIRIT AND LOVE'S FRUIT

God culminates His new relationship with the believer by placing His Spirit inside the believer. God places the Holy Spirit inside of us to reveal His love toward us. The love that the Holy Spirit reveals in the believer produces fruit. The presence of the Holy Spirit empowers the believer. The Holy Spirit enables you to stand. He gives you the provisions to keep us from falling. His power supplies you with the ability to do anything. Through His empowerment a conqueror you become, full of the fullness of God!

"If ye love me, keep my commandments and I will pray the Father, and he shall give you another comforter, that he may abide with you forever" John 14:15 & 16 (KJV), In the Greek, the word "comforter" is parakletos. Parakletos means; "one called alongside to help." The Amplified version states; *"And I will ask the Father, and He will give you another comforter (Counselor, Helper, Intercessor, Advocate, Strengthener and Standby) that He may remain in you forever."* The Holy Spirit is one called alongside us to Counsel us in the ways of love. He is here to help

us in the ways of love. He is our Intercessor and Advocate when we need Love's provisions. He is our Strengthener and Standby to love.

The counsel of God is the mind of God. When you were in High School, you were sent to the Guidance counselor. He counseled you telling you what you needed to meet your academic goals. The counselor would look at your records. From those records, he would tell you what academic career options you could take. The counselor would also, help you to find a college or trade school that would suit your circumstances and or needs. The Holy Spirit does the same for us in the spirit. Only the Holy Spirit counseling is geared towards the mind of God (Love). 1 Cor. 2:9-12 tell us,

"But on the contrary, as the Scripture says, What eye has not seen, and ear has not heard, and has not entered into the heart of man, [all that], God has prepared—made and keeps ready—for those who love Him [that is, for those who hold Him in affectionate reverence, promptly obeying Him and gratefully recognizing the benefits He has bestowed]. Yet to us God has unveiled and revealed them by and through His Spirit, for the (Holy) Spirit searches diligently, exploring and examining everything, even sounding the profound and bottomless things of God—the divine counsels and things hidden and

beyond man's scrutiny. For what person perceives (knows and understands) what passes through a man's thoughts except the man's own spirit within him? Just so no one discerns (comes to know and comprehend) the thoughts of God except the Spirit of God. Now we have not received the spirit (that belongs to) the world, but the (Holy) Spirit Who is from God, [given to us] that we might realize and comprehend and appreciate the gifts (of divine favor and blessing so freely and lavishly) bestowed on us by God." (Amplified Version)

The Holy Spirit is here to reveal the divine counsel of God. That is a promise to those who love, obey, and reverence Him. Verse 11 makes it clear that we cannot comprehend the thoughts of God, except through the Holy Spirit. What are the thoughts of God? His thoughts are His words. Jesus is the Word. Jesus is the expressed image of love. So, God's thoughts are of love. Some might say that cannot be. God has wrath that will pour on the wicked. Yes, that is true but God's judgment is of love. If He wouldn't judge sin, then His love could not be perfect.

Most people read the book of Revelation as a horror story. A story of doom and gloom. On the contrary, it is one of love. A book of compassion, protection, nurturing, marriage, longsuffering and so much more. You cannot get around it. God's love is in everything he does, think, or purposes. The Holy Spirit will cause you to realize these truths as you exercise love. For God's thoughts is not in man's wisdom. God has given us the Holy Spirit that we would understand and realize His thoughts and appreciate the gifts of divine favor and blessing in love.

No matter what, you need to apply love to your life. Whether the need is in certain areas of your life or, in circumstances you have never been in. The Holy Spirit is there to guide you in applying love in those areas. He will instruct you how to apply love in any situation of life. ***"For as many as are led by the Spirit of God, they are the sons of God."*** Rom. 8:14 (KJV). Remember, those that love are born of God (1 John 4:7).

The Spirit will lead you to love because; you are born of (God) Love. As you, mature in love your life bears fruits of love.

"But the fruit of the (Holy) Spirit, [the work which His presence within accomplishes]-is love, joy (Gladness), peace, patience (an even temper, forbearance), kindness, goodness (benevolence), faithfulness (meekness, humility gentleness, self-control (Self-restraint, continence). Against such things there is no law [that can bring a charge]. Gal. 5:22-23. (Amplified Version)

Not only does love produce love, it also produces joy. We know the Joy of the Lord is our strength (Neh. 8:10). In the New Testament, joy and might are the same words in the Greek. The Greek word is "dunamus" and it means miraculous power, explosive power, a worker of miracles. Love produces explosive, miraculous power through the Holy Spirit in us.

Love produces peace through the counsel of the Holy Spirit. All of this is because the Holy Spirit reveals the love of God, which tells you of His divine favor (1Cor. 2:12).

Knowing what God thinks of you gives you peace. Fretting is no longer a consideration. For what He did for Jesus, He will do for you. He loves you that much!

Love produces patience as the Holy Spirit stands by us. The Holy Spirit reinforces love never fails. The wait is insignificant when we know He will not fail us. Let us look at Rom. 5:1-5,

"Therefore, since we are justified—acquitted, declared righteous, and given a right standing with God—through faith, let us [grasp the fact that we] have [the peace of reconciliation] to hold and to enjoy, peace with God through our Lord Jesus Christ, the Messiah, the Anointed One. Through Him also we have [our] access (entrance, introduction) by faith into this

grace—state of God's favor—in which we [firmly and safely] stand. And let us rejoice and exult in our hope of experiencing and enjoying the glory of God. Moreover—let us also be full of joy now! Let us exult and triumph in our troubles and rejoice in our sufferings, knowing the pressure and affliction and hardship produce patient and unswerving endurance. and endurance (fortitude) develops maturity of character—that is, approved faith and tried integrity. 0And character [of this sort] produces [the habit of] joyful and confident hope of eternal salvation. Such hope never disappoints or deludes or shames us, for God's love has been poured out in our hearts through the Holy Spirit Who has been given to us." (Amplified Version)

This scripture shows through love, you will never be disappointed. You will experience no shame when you walk in love. An awakening to these truths will cause you to be full of joy [strength] now. Joy causes you to triumph in tribulations. You can endure tribulations when you are full of the strength of love. The endurance makes your hope confident of deliverance (salvation).

How is this accomplished? God accomplishes this through pouring His love into your heart by the Holy Spirit. Isn't that exciting? You can live the life of the Father. There is no weapon formed against you that can prosper (Isa. 54:17). You are more than a conqueror (Rom.8:37). All of this is because the Holy Spirit was given to you, to reveal and pour out God's love. This is the life of the spirit. God wants you deeply rooted and grounded in love. When you are rooted and grounded in love, tribulation will have no affect on your relationship with God.

Loving through adversity

My wife and I decided to have our home remodeled and have another section added to accommodate our growing family. We sought the Lord as to whom we should get to do the job. We had no knowledge of any contractors in the area. We saw names of contractors in the newspapers. We set up appointments with several of them. Some kept their appointments and others did not. Until this point, we had no confirmation in our spirit to choose one of the contractors we met.

One night at Bible study, in our home, one couple stated they were going into business for themselves. I inquired what type of business they planned to start. Their reply was "Home Improvements." We thought this is an answer to prayer. We set a time to meet with them and discuss with them what we wanted done. We were very comfortable with them. They assured us that all was in order concerning their business. My wife and I prayed, and believed the Lord gave us the confirmation that they were the ones to do the job. Starting the work made us excited. In addition, having a believer doing the work added even more excitement.

As time went on occurrences began to happen that grew progressively worse. When the project was near completion, we saw that we had a real problem. We had paid the contractor already and what was unfolding before our eyes was unreal.

We had a skylight installed upstairs and it leaked badly. The drywall installation looked like someone intoxicated had installed it. They were holes in my downstairs ceiling were someone's foot had gone through the freshly painted ceiling. The kitchen and family room ceilings and walls were wet from the leaky skylight upstairs. We called the contractor several times in effort to resolve the problems. Our calls went unanswered. The occurrences mentioned are just a few trials we had to resolve.

It got so bad my wife and I would have to laugh. We called what we saw happening in and to our home "Nightmare on Hamilton Street!" After saying that, we would laugh until we couldn't laugh anymore.

We were not going to let the devil steal our joy. Our laughing was our statement of faith. Love (God) will not allow my wife and I to experience shame. We did not focus on the circumstances. We focused on the love of God. For us, the real issue wasn't what happened to us or the money we spent. The issue was how we were going to handle it. We chose to be as God would have us to be love. With all the love we had inside we poured it out unto the contractor and his wife. My wife and I knew that no matter what came about with the house we were going to walk in love. Our resolve was to maintain our love relationship with our brother and sister in the Lord. We understood that material things did not compare to the law of the life of love. The problems didn't end. Love didn't fail!

Our relationship is stronger today than it was before we started construction. That couple consider my wife and I, their closest brother and sister in the Lord.

This is by far the most troubling situations that my wife and I had to face. When we chose to love, the Holy Spirit began to pour love out inside us. The love of God caused joy to come. Joy came when in all appearances there was nothing to be joyous about. Thanks to the Holy Spirit. The hardship meant nothing when considering how God felt about us. Love enabled us to endure. We endured because God poured out His love. God poured His Love out both to us and through us. We experienced no shame. God would not allow it. This is because our choice to love. Our choice allowed God to demonstrate His love to us. Every problem came to a resolution. Every area of the remolding worked out better than expected.

A few weeks later, the carpenter came over to allow the Lord to minister to him through my wife and I. He suffered from depression due to all the trouble he caused us. He felt like a failure. His business failed and now he is working for someone else in the same line of business. All of this strained financially. We spoke to him about the love of God. The Lord instructed me to lay my hands on him and pray that he experience His love.

If I ever meet someone with a gentle heart he was surely one, yet he was hurting inside. He saw himself as a failure in every area of his life. The Spirit of the Lord came up upon me and I began to proclaim the Word of the Lord unto him. I told him that when I put my hands on him the love of God would flood his soul. I did what He (God) told me to do. God did what He said He would do. That dear brother experienced the love of God in his soul.

I spoke with him a week later. His life had changed. A few days after this experiencing the Love of God, he was praising God. Suddenly, he began to speak in tongues as the spirit gave him utterance. Some would say this is not for today. I am not arguing this point but, to say that it was his desire. This was something he was seeking God for and what I prophesied to him would happen. God gave him the desires of his heart. No longer did he see himself a failure, he saw himself loved of God. Not only did God change the circumstances of our construction project. He changed the life of the person who worked on the project. God established a bond that couldn't be broken. Now that is the love of God!

Through this experience, the Holy Spirit showed us that love must be our foundation. With this foundation of love, there is no victory that we could not attain. Praise God! Love will produce fruit in our life that will cause us to triumph always in Christ Jesus. That is the life God lives and that life is given to us. Having our soul rooted and grounded in love produces fruit. The fruit that we produce through love brings us to the God kind of life. Eternal Life is the God kind of life. We have Eternal Life through receiving, giving and living love.

Chapter III

Eternal Life: The Product Of Love

There is a product of love that reaches further than our hearts can imagine. Eternal Life is a surety in the believer who lives the life of love. Eternal Life is not a quantity of life. God created man as eternal beings and will exist forever. For some that existence is not life it is death. Eternal Life is the quality of life that God lives. The believer who lives the life of love has the quality of life that God lives. This quality of life will affect the quantity of life that the believer has now. The life of love gives the believer the victory over death!

"This is because I have never spoken on My own authority or of My accord or self-appointed, but the Father Who has sent Me has Himself given Me orders what to say and what to tell. And I know that His commandment is (means) Eternal Life. So what ever I speak, I am saying [exactly] what My Father has told Me to say and in accordance with His instructions." John 12:49-50 (Amplified Bible).

Jesus clearly states that He has received a commandment of the Father. This commandment means Eternal Life. What is this commandment? In John 13:34, Jesus said, *"A new commandment I give unto you, that ye love one another as I have loved you, that ye also love one another."* We know that whatever Jesus spoke was the Father's commandment. John 14:31, *"But that the world may know that I love the Father, and, as the Father gave me commandment, even so I do. Arise, let us go from here."*

Jesus reinforces that His commandment is for the Body to love one another. John 15:12, *"This is my commandment, that ye love one another, as I have loved you."* Jesus spoke this after establishing Himself as the example of love [verses 9 & 10]. Jesus said, the same love the Father loved Him with He (Jesus) loves us. Additionally, Jesus tells the believer to continue in His love. If we keep Jesus' commandment, we will abide in His love. Let us go back to Jesus' previous statement, *"His commandment is (means) Eternal Life."* Jesus is telling us, when we have love one towards another. Our Action of love means **Eternal Life**. To love as Jesus loved, is to seize Eternal Life.

In 1 John 5:11-12, which this chapter is about love, states

"And this record, that God hath given to us eternal life, and this life is in his Son. He that hath the Son hath life and he that hath not the Son of God hath not life."(KJV)

To have the Son is to obtain life. To have love is to embody life. How do you acquire the Son? You have the Son by keeping His commandment. What is His commandment? His commandment is to love one another as He has loved us. This is not the legalism this is liberty. You received this ability to love when you were Born Again. Living the life of love is a result of keeping Jesus in your heart.

Jesus is the expressed image of God (Heb. 1:3). Thus, Jesus is the expressed image of Love. When you lay hold and become the expressed image of Love, you have the life of the Father.

Jesus, clearly, gave us an example of what having Him means in the 11th chapter of John. Jesus was on His way to see Mary and Martha because Lazarus was ill. On the way there, Martha came to meet Jesus. She said to Him if He would have come earlier her brother would not have died. Jesus told Martha her brother will live again. Martha replies, she knows that in the resurrection he will live again. In verses 25 & 26 of John chapter 11 we have this statement;

"Jesus said unto her, I am the resurrection, and the life he that believeth in me, though he were died, yet shall he live. And whosoever liveth and believeth in me shall never die. Believest thou this?" (KJV)

If you live (abide) and believe in Jesus, you will never die. We know that all believers have or will encounter physical death. Therefore, Jesus could not be speaking of physical death when He said you would never die. If, Jesus is not referring to physical death, what does Jesus statement mean? It means, you will live (abide) in Jesus. If, you keep His commandment to love. Get hold of Eternal Life (the life of God) and you will never die (never experience separation from Him and His Love)! Do you believe this?

In verses 35 & 36, we have this account *"Jesus wept. Then said the Jews, Behold how He loved him!"* Verse 42 & 43 Jesus said *"And I knew that Thou hearest Me always but, because of the people who stand by I said it, that they may know that Thou hast sent Me."(KJV)*

Jesus showed all the people around Him. How much love He has for those who believe. Due to His love, He will raise those who believe from the dead. In addition, it will cause them that look upon believers, to believe that the Father sent Jesus. Jesus is teaching us that we must love beyond death. We must love beyond anything that will place limits on our life of love.

Jesus confirmed this when He raised Lazarus from the dead. Jesus in His prayer to the Father stated; it is through Their oneness, we may be one in Them. So, the world may know and believe the Father sent Jesus. Let us look at John 17:21-22 (NKJV);

"that they all may be one, as You, Father, are in Me, and I in You; that they also may be one in Us, that the world may believe that You sent Me. And the glory which You gave Me, I have given them, that they may be one just as We are one:"

Therefore, through love we experience oneness with God. Love will bear witness to others that God sent us. The world will know Jesus is the love sent from God and the love that is God. Remember, the new intimacy we talked about in Chapter 1? That intimacy is the oneness I am speaking of here. This intimacy goes beyond physical death. Being born of love and having the Holy Spirit inside makes it impossible not to live the life of love. Why is it impossible? Because, you have the Holy Spirit pouring into your heart love. If, anyone ceases to live the life of love. They are no longer a believer and is spiritually dead.

In 1 John 3:14 & 15, John declares;

"We know that we have passed from death unto life, because we love the brethren. He that loveth not his brother abideth in death. Whosoever hateth his brother is a murderer and ye know that no murderer hath Eternal Life abiding in him."(KJV)

The absence or separation from life is death. The absence of love for the Body of Christ is death. When the believer leaves the way of love. He leaves the place where He abides, life. The person who does not love his brother abides in death. It is strong language that John used in verses 13 & 14. Yet, we must understand why he used this type of language. As love produces life in those who walk in love. Therefore, hate produce death in those who walk in hatred. This is why the person who walks in bitterness is a murderer. He is a murderer, due to the causing of others to receive his hatred, which is a product of death.

Now it becomes more apparent. How there are so many believers who die prematurely. Paul tells us the reason some are sickly and die prematurely. The reason is when believers do not discern the Lord's body.

"For he who eats and drinks in an unworthy manner eats and drinks judgment to himself, not discerning the Lord's body. For this reason many are weak and sick among you, and many sleep." 1 Corinthians 11:29-30 (NKJV)

Let us examine the twofold meaning of these two verses. We are the Lord's body and we must determine how we walk towards one another. Second, He is referring to the death of Christ and discerning His body as our New Testament. The New Testament is the life of love, which is given unto us. God's gift of love is Jesus. Jesus swallowed up death and gave life to those who will receive it. Therefore, we can live and give the life of love. Eternal Life is what you receive, reveal, and give. This happens when you live the life of love. When people say you are living this life, you are manifesting God. That is (Zoe) Eternal Life! If you go back to some of the other scriptures quoted in Chapters 1&2, the life of love (producing Eternal Life) in you will produce a stronger revelation in your soul.

Love's Power over Death

There is something the God desires for me to share with you concerning Love's power over death. What I am about to share, I have only shared it with a few people. I share this struggling within myself. It is so personal and overwhelming to me that it makes it very difficult to speak about. Some might think it crazy. Others might think it not true. Oh, but it is so real! I pray that you receive this truth.

One day, I received a call from a dear brother, a fellow minister. He informed me that his brother had just died. I knew something was going on spiritually for I was lead to pray all morning. I knew that God had wanted me to go there immediately. John said to me; "God told him to tell me and that I was to come." Know that God always confirms his word. At that time, I thought John did not know my purpose of coming. Later, I learned he did know why God wanted me to come. He had a dream beforehand, describing the events that were about to take place.

It was an hour ride from where I was to his house. The whole time while driving, I prayed. I was anticipating something of which I had no idea. When I arrived, we then proceeded to the hospital. Once we arrived, he arranged for us to see the body. While waiting, I asked the Lord "What do you want me to?" God said to me "You are to raise him from the dead." Immediately, the power of God came on me in such great measure. I felt like I was on fire all over my body, especially my hands. I did not hurt nor was it uncomfortable. In that moment, I felt supercharged and full of power.

We headed for the basement of the hospital. That is where they held the body. Suddenly, I knew John knew what was going on. We couldn't dare talk about it. He spoke to someone about seeing the body. Then the orderly pulled out the body from what appeared a refrigerated area. They left us alone with the body of his brother. I thought of all the prayers that I had prayed God would use me of as the apostles were. I also, thought of what was happening spiritually.

Boldness rose up inside of me as I prayed concerning my friend's brother. I touched the body it was cold and lifeless. As I began to pray, the body began to get warm. Then God spoke to me and said, "Blow on Him." I did as He said. The warm body got warmer and his mouth opened! Yes, God opened his mouth. I will not forget looking at that open mouth and seeing saliva. Almost instantly, I felt like all the demons of hell had gathered against me. The pressure was unbelievable.

My friend left the room due to the demonic pressure and him not wanting to hinder what God was doing. I understood why and we did not exchange much dialog. I went back to praying and fighting against the demonic activity. Never in my life had I experienced such demonic activity. It was as if there were a thousand voices crammed into my mind. It was so vivid. I remember as though it happened yesterday. I could hear demons saying: *"He's dead." "That's a dead man." "What are you doing?" "Are you crazy? He's dead already."* I recall one voice that rose up above the rest and said: *"What if someone sees you?" "If you do this, the press and television will mob you." "You cannot handle what will happen if, you raise him up."* Through this God was still speaking to me what to do.

God said to me "Climb on top of the table, put your lips on his lips and breath in him. Command him to rise and I will raise him up." Now I understood why his mouth opened. Until this point everything God told me to do, I did and he produced results in each occurrence. As I proceeded to climb on the cart, the demonic pressure was now unbearable to my body. The demonic voices became more desperate and louder in my head. I heard one of the many voices say "are you going to put your lips on a dead man?" Those words hit me to my core. Still proceeding climbing on the cart I heard another voice say, "What if someone inters the room and see you on top of a dead man! They will take you away in a strait jacket."

By this time, I had pressed forward and was face to face with the deceased brother. I looked down and saw saliva in his open mouth. That is when I stopped. I thought well if I blew in his mouth, it is the same thing. Therefore, I blew in his mouth. Again, God repeated what he desired for me to do. I could not bring myself to put my lips on the deceased lips. You might say I don't blame you for not doing that. I realized afterwards that it was a small price to pay to obey God.

The physical demonic pressure did not subside. I knew that I had failed my brother and I failed God. I walked out, proceeded to the hospital chapel, and prayed to the father concerning my failure. Even then, the demonic pressure was still tremendous. Regardless to all the pressure, there was no doubt in my mind and heart that God would have raised him up. Only if I was obedient to what he instructed me to do. I looked over at John and he was in utter amazement to what he had just beheld. I talked to him about some of the events that took place (Other things did not come out until we discussed much later.) He said it amazed him that I went that far.

The Lord led me to apologize to John and ask for forgiveness, for my failure to love completely and unconditionally.

I tried to understand what all of this meant. Then God brought to my recollection that I wanted to know him in the power of his resurrection. I did not know (revelation knowledge) that the power of his resurrection was "Love." The Lord let me know there were seeds, which He planted in me. Now, He was calling upon the fruit of those seeds. Those seeds were revelations of His Love. The Problem was I was not ready or willing to apply that Love in every area of my life, even death. Love has total victory over death. I learned that we must love beyond death. That love must go beyond anything that will place limits on our life. What can separate us from the Love of God? Romans 8:35-39 tells us;

"Who (what) shall separate us from the love of Christ? shall tribulation, or distress, or persecution, or famine, or nakedness, or peril, or sword? As it is written, For thy sake we are killed all the day long we are accounted as sheep for the slaughter. Nay, in all these things we are more than conquerors through him that loved us. For I am persuaded, that neither <u>death</u>, nor life, nor angels, nor principalities, nor powers, nor things present, nor things to come, Nor height, nor depth, nor any other creature,

shall be able to separate us from the love of God, which is in Christ Jesus our Lord." (KJV)

I implore you my brother and my sister, to apply this love to every area that is life and even physical death. Then you will know total victory. We have total victory over physical death also, because we dwell in Love. For when we experience physical death, we will never experience separation from God. Therefore, death has no power and the grave has no sting!

If you are one, in the Lord, who desires to do great exploits, then you must pay a price. That price is complete love applied to every area of your life. 1 John 5:13-15 states;

"These things have I written unto that believe on the name of the Son of God that ye may know that ye have Eternal Life, and that ye may believe on the name of the Son of God. And this is the confidence that we have in Him, that, if we ask any thing according to His will, He heareth us: and if we know that He hear us, whatsoever we ask, we know that we have the petitions that we desired of Him." (KJV)

When you walk in love toward others as Jesus did, the Father will always hear you.

Because, He dwells in you and you dwell in Him. You have the life of Jesus. You have the life of the Father. In the Father's life, there is no death. Love gives you that life. Eternal Life is to know the Father.

"And this is eternal life, that they may know You, the only true God, and Jesus Christ whom You have sent." John 17:3 (NKJV)

To know the Father is to know love.

"Beloved, let us love one another, for love is of God; and everyone who loves is born of God and knows God."

1 John 4:7 (NKJV).

How wonderful is the love that is God. That Love produces oneness, the substance of God, sanctification, righteousness, Joy, peace, absolute understanding of God (in our life), and Eternal Life.

When a believer takes hold of these truths, he begins to manifest the life of God. As he, walks in this love the believer's nature and character changes to that which is Gods. No, you never lose your personality in God. You maintain your personality with the life of God. God's character and nature perfects your personality. Love removes all the flaws in any personality. It is Love that makes you perfect!

"Though I speak with the tongues of men and of angels, but have not love, I have become sounding brass or a clanging cymbal. And though I have the gift of prophecy, and understand all mysteries and all knowledge, and though I have all faith, so that I could remove mountains, but have not love, I am nothing. And though I bestow all my goods to feed the poor, and though I give my body to be burned, but have not love, it profits me nothing. Love suffers long and is kind; love does not envy; love does not parade itself, is not puffed up; does not behave rudely, does not seek its own, is not provoked, thinks no evil; does not rejoice in iniquity, but rejoices in the truth; bears all things, believes all things, hopes all things, endures all things. Love never fails. But whether there are prophecies, they will fail; whether there are tongues, they will cease; whether there is knowledge, it will vanish away. For we know in part and we prophesy in part. But when that which is perfect has come, then that which is in part will be done away. When I was a child, I spoke as a child, I understood as a child, I thought as a child; but when I became a man, I put away childish things. For now we see in a mirror, dimly, but then face to face. Now I know in part, but then I shall know just as I also am known. And now abide faith, hope, love, these three; but the greatest of these is love." 1corintians 13:1-13(NKJV)

The life of love will make 1 Corinthians 13 a statement of your life. It will be said of you, He suffers long and is kind; He envies not; He vaunt not himself, he is not puffed up; he does not behave himself unseemly, he seeks not his own, he is not easily provoked, he thinks no evil; he rejoices not in iniquity, but rejoices in the truth; he bears all things, believes all things, hopes all things, and endures all things. **HE NEVER FAILS!**

Isn't that the life of God? Thanks are to God, it is your life also. That is if you choose to love as Jesus loved us. Jesus came that we would have life and that more abundantly. Love produces abundance of life! That abundance of life is illustrated in John 4:9-14

"Then saith the woman of Samaria unto him, How is it that thou, being a Jew, askest drink of me, who am a woman of Samaria? For the Jews have no dealings with the Samaritans. Jesus answered, and said unto her, If thou knewest the gift of God, and who it is that saith of thee, Give me to drink, thou wouldest have asked of him, and he would have given thee living water. The woman saith unto him, Sir, thou hast nothing to draw with, and the well is deep from where, then hast thou that living water? Art thou greater than our father, Jacob, who gave us the well, and drank from it himself, and his children, and his

cattle? Jesus answered and said unto her, Whosoever drinketh of this water shall thirst again But whosoever drinketh of the water that I shall give him shall never thirst, but the water that I shall give him shall be in him a well of water springing up into everlasting life."

(KJV) We have already established that love produces everlasting life. The woman at the well example is a powerful statement of being born of love and what love will produce. Jesus knew that the woman at the well needed real love. She had five husbands and the one she was with was not her husband. Jesus offered her a drink of water. Jesus told her, if she would drink. She would never thirst again. Jesus also said, it would spring up to everlasting life. Everlasting life flowing inside those who drink it. Love will spring up out of us to everlasting life.

Some would say that He in speaking of the spring is speaking of the Holy Ghost. I agree that He is.

"Now hope does not disappoint, because the love of God has been poured out in our hearts by the Holy Spirit who was given to us." Rom. 5:5 (NKJV)

The amplified version reads; *"For God's love has been poured out in our hearts through the Holy Spirit."* God's love flows inside of us outward like spring unto Eternal Life. Jesus said it would be that way in John 7:37 & 38

"In the last day, that great day of the feast, Jesus stood and cried out, saying, if any man thirst, let him come unto me, and drink. He that believeth on me, as the scripture hath said, out of his belly shall flow rivers of living water."(KJV)

The Greek word used in this verse for "belly" is koilia. Koilia refers to the heart, belly and womb. Jesus clarified how the water spring up out of our heart. He said it would flow like a river! Love flowing out of us like a river—that is the life of God. **As a river moves the earth around it, so does love move our flesh**. We must expect that we would feel that love in our flesh. I am not saying we walk by our feelings. I am saying it is God's will that we experience his love in body, soul, and spirit. If you don't experience it, how can you manifest that love to someone else? No one can walk beyond his or her knowledge. This is why the manifestation of God's love in the believer is rare.

Very few believers have experienced love in the whole person of man. Jesus promised in John 14:21, that the love of God will be manifested to those that love him and keep His commandment. It is not a maybe. It is a fact. Jesus said He would show Himself to you! Do you believe that He will? If so, it will be a reality to you. The Holy Spirit will pour love out upon your flesh and soul as well as in your spirit, which will spring outward unto Eternal Life. Nothing shall separate us from the love of Christ.

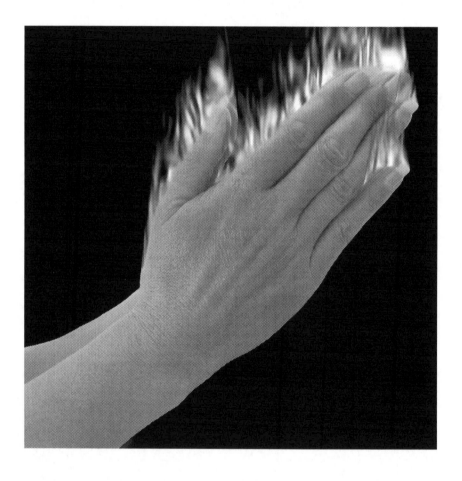

CHAPTER IV

THE HOLY SPIRIT AND FIRE

There is a fire of the Holy Spirit. His fire burns in the heart of the believer (Luke 3:16).

That fire is love. It causes the believer to be faithful to the Father. This fire constrains our flesh.

"For the love of Christ compels us, because we judge thus: that if One died for all, then all died;" 2 cor. 5:14 (NKJV)

It is the writings of God's love [His Word] on our hearts. Hebrews 8:10-11 tells us;

"For this is the covenant that I will make with the house of Israel after those days, saith the Lord ; I will put my law into their mind, and write them in their hearts: and I will be to them a God, and they shall be to me a people: and they shall not teach every man his neighbor, and every man his brother, saying, know the Lord: for all shall know me, from the least to the greatest." (KJV)

God said the law; He will write on our heart is His covenant with us. God said all would know Him because of the writings of

His law on our hearts. What is the law that He has written on our hearts? That law is the commandment of love spoke of in the previous chapter. The commandment of love when written on our hearts by God is His fire. This fire must is a separate experience than the filling of the Holy Ghost (Spirit). Some denominations it is known as the Baptism of the Holy Ghost (Spirit). If they were not separate, the Holy Spirit would not have inspired John the Baptist to say: ***"He shall baptize you with the Holy Ghost AND FIRE."*** Luke 3:16 (KJV). That doesn't mean the two cannot happen simultaneously. For it happened that way on the day of Pentecost.

"When the Day of Pentecost had fully come, they were all with one accord in one place. And suddenly there came from heaven, a sound of a rushing mighty wind, and it filled the whole house where they were sitting. Then there appeared to them divided tongues, as of Fire, and one sat upon each of them. And they were all filled with the Holy Spirit and began to speak with other tongues, as the Spirit gave them utterance." Act 2:1-4 [NKJV]

Divided tongues appeared unto them as of **FIRE**. Moreover, it sat upon each of them. They all received the fire of God. How do we know they received the fire of God? They manifested it. In verses 44 & 45, it is clearly seen.

"And all that Believed were together, and had all things common and sold their possessions and goods, and parted them to men, as every man had need."(KJV)

Today, the church buildings are full of believers. What is the difference between then and now? The body of believers are not together (united) and have everything in common. Only the fire of God can purge and blend our hearts into a homogeneous mass. It is the fire of God that can make our possessions the possessions of those who need. The fire of love takes selfishness and consumes it with giving. Not leaving a trace of selfishness to those who look upon it. This fire is necessary for us, the body of Christ, to become unified in our faith. We need the fire for us to put our last enemy—death—under our feet. We need the fire for us say that we are ready for the Lord's return!

How I long to see the fire of God burn through the body of Christ. **God's fire will cause barriers to fall, and differences to dissolve. God's fire will cause religious denominations to disappear. All of this will happen due to the fire of love.** The fire of love will confirm to the world we are His disciples.

I hear so much about revival. "Let us pray for revival" "We need revival" "Revival is moving through the land" are some of the proclamations made. God has no interest in revival. He is interested in us being one as He is one with Jesus. Many preachers are in love with the idea of revival. We create services and called them "revival meetings." The meetings are to produce a state of euphoria in the hearts and minds of the believers. I am not saying that the intentions are not right. The methods are producing short-lived experiences. When God writes on the hearts and souls of believers the fire of love is it is a life experience. **God wants us to go further than a revived state of being.** He desires that we be full of the fullness of Him, love. Yes, I believe there will be another great move of God before Jesus returns. That move will be the pouring out of God's fullness upon all flesh.

In order to get filled with the fire of God, you must be honest with yourself about your relationship with God. Do you believe that God's word is true? Do you believe that His promises are for you? Do you believe God has a good opinion of you? Do you believe God's commitment to make you as he is in this world? If you believe these truths, your faith will cause you to receive His fire. I had no idea what it would be like to experience the fire of God. All I knew this is what I wanted. I knew of no teachings on how to receive His fire. So, I prayed to receive the fire of the Holy Spirit. I prayed as if I wanted to receive salvation or the filling of the Holy Spirit. I wasn't conscious I had received it until God spoke to my heart and said I had received it. It was through this experience that I am about to share. How God spoke to my heart that I received His fire.

I had a preaching engagement in Plainfield, N.J. on a Sunday evening. What I saw in this church that troubled me to the core of my soul. I had preached there before and knew the condition of the hearts there. For the Holy Spirit moved mightily concerning their relationship with the Lord. Unaware, this time things were worse than anyone could have imagined.

As I sat in the pulpit, I saw people talking aloud as though they were at a baseball game. When it was time to receive the tithes and offerings, the call to give sounded like a commercial. "Dig deep down in your pockets and pull out dollars!" "No change!" "Give until it hurts!" exclaimed one of the preachers. My heart went out to the congregation for I knew they were financially strained. The financial hardships were due to the demands placed on them by the church.

As the choir began to sing, the person who invited me told me not to preach very long. To my right, I saw one of the ministers dancing, street dances one would see on television. There was a spirit of worldliness like I have never seen before in any church. All of the young women had babies and were single. The Holy Spirit revealed to me that the youth had to go to church services geared towards adults. So they (the youth), created an environment at the church that satisfied their desires to meet people, date, and experiment with sex. The adults allowed this environment to persist. By this time, I was almost in shock! The whole experience played out like a Hollywood production of how the world views the church.

As I began to preach, the resistance to the Word was enormous. I could feel the anointing beginning to lift and then it would come upon me again. People were still walking around and talking as though it was a social event. I wanted to stop but the Holy Spirit said, "No." I could not understand why he wanted me to continue. There were words the Holy Spirit had me to say that I didn't understand until after the message was over and other occurrences took place.

It was the longest half of hour message I have ever preached. It felt as though I was speaking for at least 2 hours. After sitting down, they preceded to go into a second service. In this part of the service, the church was broken up into groups. The groups had to give account whether the group met their financial goals. Those who didn't meet their goals experienced public ridicule and displayed as failures. Inside I was hurting inside. Because, I knew it hurt many of the members badly, through the whole ordeal. You could see it on their faces.

Instantly, I saw the Church of Sardis.

"And to the angel of the church in Sardis write, 'These things says He who has the seven Spirits of God and the seven stars: "I know your works, that you have a name that you are alive, but you are dead. Be watchful, and strengthen the things which remain, that are ready to die, for I have not found your works perfect before God. Remember therefore how you have received and heard; hold fast and repent. Therefore if you will not watch, I will come upon you as a thief, and you will not know what hour I will come upon you. You have a few names even in Sardis who have not defiled their garments; and they shall walk with Me in white, for they are worthy. He who overcomes shall be clothed in white garments, and I will not blot out his name from the Book of Life; but I will confess his name before My Father and before His angels. "He who has an ear, let him hear what the Spirit says to the churches." Rev. 3:1-6 (NKJV)

I saw it like never before. In my mind, I thought the church's condition was because they were trying and somehow they just missed it. God revealed to me, that I was wrong. The Church at Sardis did not miss it. God revealed that they did not even trying to seek Him. I saw the church in Plainfield condition the same condition as the Church of Sardis. The realization of this was horrifying to me.

The Fire—God's Love and Compassion on your body

This picture stayed in my mind for three days. I could not get any release in my spirit concerning that church. I cried, for three days straight. I would pray over and over for them. On Wednesday night, I was in Bible study and the group prayed as a whole about the church. It was then I got a release in my spirit of my burden for the church. After that prayer was when the Holy Spirit spoke to my heart "You received the fire." The words God spoke resonated in me. He spoke "rhema" (living words/revelation) to my heart. I saw how fire moved me with compassion that consumed my whole person. The church wasn't just another church but they were my people. They were dead and I felt the loss. I realized why God sent me there. I understood why I went through this traumatic experience. From the time, God spoke to my heart that His fire was there. The love of God is more real to me than I could have ever thought possible. When the revelation came I felt Gods love in my flesh as though He had personally put his arms around me and embraced me. Even more so, that love flowed out of me to others in a greater dimension. For, example I would hug a brother or a sister and they would fall out under the power of that love. This happens with me more times than not.

My desire for you, my brother and my sister, is that you experience that fire of love burning in your heart. It will move you in ways untold. The tangible presence of God will be great on your life.

In Isaiah 4:4, the Lord said He would wash away all the filth and purge our blood by the Spirit of Justice (or Righteousness) and by the **Spirit of BURNING**.

"Above all things have <u>fervent</u> love among yourselves for love shall <u>cover</u> the multitude of sins." 1 Peter 4:8 (KJV)

The word fervent in the Greek is "ektenes" and means intent—without ceasing. The Amplified Bible reads;

"Above all things have intense and unfailing love for one another, for love covers a multitude of sins—forgives and disregards the offenses of others."

Our love should be ablaze towards our brothers and sisters in Christ. For fire is a source of power. As fire is in the natural so is the fire of God in the spiritual. The fire of love will purge the sins (plural) of those that are among you. That fire will touch the lives of all that you meet. **God is a consuming fire.**

"For our God is a consuming fire." Hebrews 12:29 (NKJV)

Remember, **"As He is so are we in this world."**

The fire of God caused my faith to take on a new dimension. I became conscious when my joy [strength] underwent an attack. My ministry became more effective. It changed the lives of my whole family. The Holy Spirit was no longer an entity. He became a person to me. I realized another person of the Godhead lives in me and continually pours God's love into my heart. For the first time since being Born of God, I knew I could do anything through Christ. Most of all I understood why God's ability was in me. With this understanding, the fire became more intense inside of me. That intensity grew because the dimensions of the love of Jesus became known unto me.

Through learning the dimensions of His love, the process of filling me with all the fullness of love began. I have an excitement that God is revealing His glory unto us—the Church.

The fire inside will cause a new intimacy with the Godhead— Father, Son, and Holy Spirit. God is intimate with our whole man— body, soul, and spirit. It is not enough for us to be intimate with the Father and the Son. That is not the whole person of God. We must be intimate with His whole person to say that we are intimate with God. Anything else would be being intimate with a part of God.

Decide to be intimate with the whole person of God. This decision is the beginning of possessing love consciousness. God decided to be intimate with your whole person and He is conscious of His love for you always. That love consciousness is the life of God. For everything God did, He did with you in mind. Jesus said He came that we would have life and it more abundantly.

"The thief cometh not, but for to steal, and to kill, and to destroy: I am come that they might have life, and that they might have it more abundantly." John 10:10 (KJV)

I pray that you choose abundant life. Yes, it is a choice. You must set your will to be intimate with the whole person of God. All God's word is for you. Will you set your will to have it in your life? I believe that you will decide to be intimate with the whole person of God. Once you have set your will than you can release your faith through love. Once you have released your faith, you will see the fire of God in your life. The fire of God will become ablaze in you! It is by faith that you receive all of Love's provisions.

CHAPTER V

FAITH WORKS BY LOVE

Though, this book is not about faith. We cannot overlook this fact. Through faith, we are recipients of the grace of God. This chapter, I pray, will change your outlook on faith. The Holy Spirit desires to change your faith from possibility faith to impossibility faith. Impossibility faith is faith that is impossible to fail!

"For [if we are] in Christ Jesus, neither circumcision nor uncircumcision counts for anything, but only faith activated and energized and expressed and working through love." Galatians 5:6. (Amplified version)

What counts for anything? Faith activated, energized, expressed and working through love. That sounds different from what we hear so many times "Just have faith, nothing is impossible to them that believe." All within us, we believe, and then failure comes. Then a brother or sister will come along tell you why you failed. "You did not exercise enough faith this or that is why your faith failed." In reality, it is love that is missing from our faith. As love is a spirit, faith is a spirit.

"We having the same spirit of faith, according as it is written, I believed, and therefore have I spoken; we also believe, and therefore speak;" 2 Cor. 4:13 (KJV)

Faith is not of the mind. It is of the spirit (pneuma) [see Chapter 1]. It must therefore, be activated in your heart (psuche)[see Chapter 1] by love. Faith must be energized in your heart (psuche) by love. Finally, expressed in your heart (psuche) by love. The believer is to understand that faith must be continually working in his heart (psuche) by love. As a switch turns on a light when turned, so does love turn faith on when love is in action. Too many times, there is an exertion of faith out of need. The need isn't the problem. It is the need motivating faith that is the problem. When Satan perceives your need(s) will motivate you, He will insure you always have a perceived need. Once the focus is off love (God) and on the need, Satan won the battle. Faith is having complete confidence in God's love towards us that whatever the need is He will provide it.

In 1 John 4:17 the word "boldness" is translated "confidence" in other scriptures. The Greek word is "parrhesia" which means; all outspokenness, frankness, bluntness, boldness of speech, assurance, confidence. With this insight, let us look at 1 John 4:17

"Herein is our love made perfect, that we may have boldness in the Day of Judgment, because as he is, so are we in this world." (KJV)

From this, we see how our love is perfect. We also see how to have confidence in God's love for us. With this confidence, we can stand in the Day of Judgment. All of these truths are possible because as He is so are we in this world.

No matter how big or small the need, it makes no difference. God will provide it because He loves us so. Faith trusts that love will perform all that is necessary. There is an established alliance between faith and love. Love has an agreement to give power to faith. To declare faith is an action of love, is saying the same. Love empowers faith. It builds faith like a house under construction. This is seen in Jude 1:20-21.

"But ye, beloved, building up yourselves on your most holy faith, praying in the Holy Ghost, Keep yourselves in the love of God, looking for the mercy of our Lord Jesus Christ unto Eternal Life." (KJV)

The Amplified expresses the verse in this manner *"Make progress, rise like an edifice higher and higher—praying in the Holy Ghost."* When we pray in the Holy Spirit, we make progress.

When we pray in the Holy Ghost, we keep ourselves in love, building our faith up like an edifice that rises higher and higher. If we are praying in the Spirit, than all that takes place, must take place in the spirit first, than it will manifest in the flesh or materially.

Faith is visible as love is visible. James said, "I will **SHOW** thee my faith by my works." What are the works he is referring to? He is referring to the works of brotherly love. James started the same chapter by describing how we should entreat our brother.

The definition of faith, when looked at in its entirety, reinforces the purposes of God concerning love consciousness. Faith's definition is Hebrews 11:1

"Now faith is the assurance (the confirmation, the title-deed) of the things [we] hope for, being the proof of things [we] do not see and the conviction of their reality—faith perceiving as real fact what is not revealed to the senses." (Amplified version) When, we put together what faith works by with the definition of faith, we get this *"Now faith activated and energized and expressed and working through love is the assurance (the confirmation, the title-deed) of things [we] hope for, being the proof-the tangibility—of things [we] do not see, and the*

conviction of their reality—faith perceiving as real fact; what is not revealed to the senses."

Love is vital. Love is the expression of our faith. Love is the proof that whatever you ask God you can receive it. Love causes your faith to perceive, the fact you have what you hope for. Even though you cannot see or touch what you are believing for.

Remember, faith is necessary to please God (Heb. 11:6). Why is faith necessary to please God? When you walk in faith, it is an act of love towards the Father. It says to the Father that you know Him and love him. If you want to please God, you must motivate your faith by love. Without love, nothing else activating your faith is faith.

Actually, nothing else can activate real faith but love.

"For whatever is not of faith is sin" Rom. 14:23. If faith works by love, then the absence of love makes it not faith. If whatever we do, say, and pray is not of faith it is sin. God is so longsuffering with us. We struggle with love and we fill ourselves with the Word of faith. As a result we there is no perfection in faith or love.

Paul tells us in the 13th Chapter of 1 Corinthians *"And though I have all faith, so that I could remove mountains, and have not*

love, I AM NOTHING." He didn't say it profited him nothing. Paul said I am nothing. Faith is the bases of everything we receive from God. Without love, there is no faith. Without faith, there is no Grace. If, there is no grace, there is no salvation. Without salvation, we are nothing. What counts for anything? Faith activated, energized, expressed and working through love counts for anything.

Faith Comes By Hearing—Love

"So, then faith cometh by hearing, and hearing by the Word of God." Romans 10:17. (KJV)

Faith works by love, but in this verse, it says that faith comes by hearing. Faith comes by hearing what? It comes by hearing the Word of God. The Greek word in used in that verse for "word" is "rhema." Rhema means the spoken Word of God. For us it would be the spoken revelation of God's Word. Let us think about something, if faith comes by hearing the spoken revelation of God's Word. Then God's Word must activate faith. We know that love activates faith. Could it be that God's spoken words are words of love? Definitely, they are words of love! That revelation is what the world is to comprehend.

When you speak the revelation of God's Word, it puts love in the activation mode for faith to come. Faith can only be expressed through love. As faith progresses (comes) it is empowered (created) and expressed through love. That is walking in the spirit! The Just shall live by faith.

"For therein is the righteousness of God revealed from faith to faith: as it is written, The just shall live by faith." Romans 1:17 (KJV)

When God pours out the fire of love into your heart by the Holy Spirit, it will set your faith a flame. A flame that you can live by and please God by.

To walk in faith, love must be at the center of your heart, mind and soul. This is why love consciousness is necessary for the believer to posses. For it enables the believer to activate, empower, express the faith that Jesus exemplified. We are to exemplify that kind of faith also. That is the God kind of faith. That is the kind of faith God is calling us to live by. Everything God purposed, He purposed with this in mind. Living as Jesus lived in this world (the expressed image of love).

Love is the victory that overcomes the world, even our faith (1 John 5:4). You see they are tied together. If you want victory that overcomes the world, than your faith must work by love. Your life must be a life of faith activated, energized, expressed and working through love. I can say this with out changing the meaning of the scripture ***"For without faith that works by love it is impossible to please God."***

Therefore, keep love as the basis of your faith and you will know victory. Your conscious will be flaming with love for the lost, your Christian family and God. As you, apply what you have read in the first five chapters. The process of love consciousness has begun in your life.

CHAPTER VI

LOVE CONSCIOUSNESS

All that I discussed up until now has laid the basis for love consciousness. Some of the scriptures that I referred to in previous chapters I will refer to again. This time I will refer to them with a different purpose. What is Love Consciousness? Some will say, "Love is always on my mind." Well love consciousness is not just having love on your mind. It is a way of life. It is being conscientious of the love life or the life of God.

Love consciousness supersedes righteous consciousness. How does this consciousness supersede righteous consciousness? Righteous consciousness eliminates sin consciousness. A soul that possesses righteous consciousness is aware there is no inferiority or shame, because God has declared you righteous. A soul that possesses love consciousness is cognizant of God's opinion of him. It is the perception in your soul of the love that God pours out into your heart. This awareness is continual. Love consciousness is knowing all you do and all that you are is of love, because you are born of love. Love consciousness is an understanding that establishes you in every area of our life through and by love.

Are you beginning to see the difference between righteous consciousness and love consciousness? Love consciousness engulfs every area of your life. When received, righteous consciousness becomes a part of love consciousness. Faith working by love is the beginning of love consciousness. You may wonder how is this so? First, we live by faith. All that we receive comes through faith. Our relationship with the whole person of God is of faith. Faith without the experience of love is dead. If you recall in Chapter V, without love, what we call faith really is not faith. Knowing love and knowing you are born of love is important. The ability to manifest love and receive love is by the Holy Spirit. It is not enough to know it you must live it. You must be continually mindful that God's character and nature is now your character and nature, [that is only if you choose it to be]. If you want to hold on to your character and your nature, you will. The Holy Spirit will not force God's character and nature on you. To choose God's character and nature will result in you knowing and experiencing the fullness of God.

God desires that you know the fullness of His love. Also, He wants you to be full of the fullness of His love (Eph. 3:19). That is to have love in your spirit, soul and body. I like to say "The fullness of God in the fullness of man." I believe that it is your desire to know the fullness of love; otherwise, you wouldn't be reading this book.

There is something the Holy Spirit is prompting me to say that puts everything that He is saying into proper perspective for the reader.

"And He said unto them, take heed what ye hear with what measure ye measure, it shall be measured to you and unto you that hear shall more be given." Mark 4:24 (KJV)

Whatever value you place on these words will be your return. I want all of God. I refuse to put limits on the God's Word. I plead with you by the Spirit of God to measure with your spirit. For the spirit is infinite and so will, your return is infinite.

Confessions of Love

"For with the heart man believeth unto righteousness and with the mouth confession is made unto salvation." Romans 10:10 (KJV)

You may think what does this have to do with love consciousness. Everything, for in our heart, righteousness becomes established through believing. With your mouth, confession brings salvation. Salvation is the all-inclusive word in the Bible. It speaks of healing, preservation, justification, redemption, grace, sanctification, forgiveness, imputation, propitiation, soundness, deliverance, prosperity, and safety.

In Acts 2:21, Peter was quoting from Joel the prophet, and used the word salvation. Joel used the word deliverance instead of salvation (Joel 2:32). This shows that the two words are interchangeable. When deliverance or salvation takes place, it is always deliverance/salvation from something or somewhere to something or somewhere. I will go into this further later on in this chapter.

As you confess God's opinion of you and His love towards you, your consciousness is awakened. Your consciousness becomes awakened, because you put the Word into your soul. The Word provokes your consciousness to love when you confess the Word.

When you hear yourselves speak the Word, the process of deliverance from sin consciousness begins. The Word is Love. That Love produces faith. Faith perceiving as real fact what is the senses cannot understand. What is the real fact that your senses cannot understand? Your senses cannot understand that you have deliverance! Deliverance to what you confess. You are confessing the Word, which is love. Therefore, love governs your actions, thoughts and motives when it takes residence in your soul.

The beautiful part about all of this is that though your senses do not perceive what is happening. The very word you confess will cause your senses to know what your spirit knows. When you confess love, it produces love. Did you get it? Confession is a statement of acceptance that God states the truth. It tells the Father and your soul that you believe whatever God has promised.

Hebrews 10:23 & 24

"Let us hold fast the profession of our faith without wavering (for He is faithful that promised) And let us consider one another to provoke unto love and to good works."(KJV)

God declares not to waver in your confession for God is faithful to His promises. As you confess, you should consider your brother in love. Remember the commandment to love one another? That is how you consider each other with your confession.

Confess that you love the body. Confess you can love and will love the body, because you are born of Love. When you confess the Word or the promises of God, you confess Jesus. Confession causes the love of God, to dwell in your soul. This comes together in 1 John 4:15 &16

"Whosoever shall confess that Jesus is the Son of God, God dwelleth in him, and he in God. And we have known and believed the love that God hath to us. God is love and he that dwelleth in love dwelleth in God, and God in him." (KJV)

One part of that verse is key; they already had known and believed the love that God had towards them. None of this will mean anything if you do not know God's opinion of you.

What is God's Opinion of Me?

You have read many times the statement where I refer to God's opinion of you. This makes everything that I said in this book personal. When you know what God thinks of you, nothing else really matters. The difficulty in illustrating God's opinion of you is the experience is through His Word. The realization of His opinion comes when His love is shown to you. I desire that I could lay my hands on all that would desire to experience His opinion. That is not possible. I am depending on the Holy Spirit to help me instruct you so you can experience His opinion of you. I know the experience is explosive and life changing. It changed my life, and others that the Lord had me to minister to personally.

First, we will look at what God says in His Word. We will look in an area that speaks of His opinion of us.

"That in the ages to come he might show the exceeding riches of his grace in his kindness toward us through Christ Jesus. For by grace are ye saved through faith and that not of yourselves: it is the gift of God." Ephesians 2:7-8 (KJV)

To see the totality of this verse we must look at the meaning of the Greek word used for "grace." In the Greek grace means; ***graciousness (as gratifying), of manner or act especially the** divine influence upon the heart, and its reflection in the life including gratitude:—acceptable, benefit, favor, gift, grace (-ious), joy, liberality, pleasure, thank (-s,—worthy). *Strong's Exhaustive Concordance of the Bible*

Going back to the verse, God's desire becomes apparent. He desires to show His favor, joy, and pleasure towards you. He wants you to know how acceptable you are to Him through His loving kindness. For it is in believing this through faith that we obtain salvation. It is a gift of God. God wants us to know that He has pleasure in us.

God longs for you to know that He has pleasure in you. God expects you to know that He benefits from your relationship with Him. God yearns for us to know that it is gratifying to Him to have this relationship. Why is it so special to God? This is because of His great love toward you and His good opinion of you. When you know that God has a good opinion of you. You will have Peace. This is a promise to the believer. *"Thou wilt keep him in perfect peace, whose mind is stayed on thee: because he trusteth in thee."* Isaiah 26:3 (KJV). Keep your mind on God's opinion of you, and you will know true liberty. When you do this, you will completely know God loves you. Furthermore, you will know nothing can take away from the relationship God has with you. For God thinks highly of you.

Romans 5:20 shows that grace is greater than sin. *"Moreover the law entered, that the offense might abound. But where sin abounded, grace did much more abound."(KJV)* God's influence upon the heart of man is greater where sin abounds! The Amplified version reads, *"Where sin abounds, grace super abounds."* God is causing His grace to abound towards you even where sin abounds. Nothing can change God's opinion of you.

God spoke this to my heart, concerning His opinion of me. He spoke this as I was teaching a group of believers. In Matthew 3:16-17 God Spoke from heaven.

"And Jesus, when He was baptized, went up straightway out of the water: and, lo, the heavens were opened unto Him, and He saw the Spirit of God descending like a dove, and lighting upon Him: And lo a voice from heaven, saying, This is my beloved Son, in whom, I am well pleased."(KJV)

The Holy Spirit said to my heart, "God speaks the same of you for you are His child."

It brought tears to my eyes to know that I pleased Him just by committing my heart to love Him. He showed me that what He felt towards me was grace. Think about it. When the Father spoke these words about Jesus, Jesus had done no works. Jesus' ministry had not yet begun. *"For by grace are ye saved through faith; and that not of yourselves: it is the gift of God: Not of works, lest any man should boast". Ephesians 2:8-9 (KJV)*

With that assurance of how God feels about you, the reality of love makes His promises more sure. For you know what a person will do in the name of love. A person who loves another would not withhold anything good. The receiving person cannot do anything to change the love of the giving person. In this Romans 8:38-39 becomes a surety.

"For I am persuaded, that neither death, nor life, nor angels, nor principalities, nor powers, nor things present, nor things to come, nor height, nor depth, nor any other creature, shall be able to separate us from the love of God, which is in Christ Jesus our Lord."(KJV)

If you have just fallen, or accused of the enemy, confess your sin(s). Come to God in love and repent. Then confess that you give pleasure to the Father. When you are attacked of the enemy, confess that God has a good opinion of you. Then watch what happens in your soul. The love of God will flood it like a deluge. Never accept depression again. Never accept feeling lonely again. Never accept anything that will keep you estranged from God. For when you speak to God about His opinion of you, He will demonstrate His opinion of you to you. He will demonstrate His opinion of you in your spirit, soul, and body. Once you have spoken to Him, you will always end that conversation satisfied. You will feel very much loved by God.

In talking with a sister about falling in sin, she explained her situation. She wanted to know how to recapture the experience. The experience when God poured His love out on her flesh. Before, the Lord had someone who I ministered the love of God to, minister it to her. I told her that the experience was a promise. John 14:21 & 20 is that promise:

"At that day ye shall know that I <am> in my Father, and ye in me, and I in you. He that hath my commandments, and keepeth them, he it is that loveth me: and he that loveth me shall be loved of my Father, and I will love him, and will manifest myself to him."(KJV)

The Lord said He would (continually) manifest Himself to her. The promise was not for one occurrence, it was unlimited. He said He would manifest Himself to her. All she needed to do was to confess His love and express her need to feel that love. Once she made her confession, the Holy Ghost, began to pour out that love to her.

I informed her grace of God is inside her, to show God's favor to her. I continued telling her that the grace inside her was the Spirit of Grace. The Holy Spirit is the Spirit of Grace. He is inside you to pour out God's grace to you or otherwise be gracious to you. I saw it in her face. It was a relief to her that she had not lost that experience forever because of sin. She experienced that love again and has moved on in God.

"What shall separate us from the love of Christ?" Rom.8:35.

Hebrews 10:29 describes grace as a Spirit.

"Of how much sorer punishment, suppose ye, shall he be thought worthy, who hath trodden underfoot the Son of God, and hath counted the blood of the covenant, wherewith he was sanctified, an unholy thing, and hath done despite unto the Spirit of grace?"(KJV)

Another example of the Spirit of grace is in Exodus 34:5-6.

"And the LORD descended in the cloud, and stood with him there, and proclaimed the name of the LORD. And the LORD passed by before him, and proclaimed, The LORD, The LORD God, merciful and gracious, longsuffering, and abundant in goodness and truth." (KJV)

God is a Spirit. God declared that He is gracious. God is not referring to an attitude. He is referring to His person. All that God is is Spirit. His Spirit is inside us. The Holy Spirit is that Spirit of Grace who lives in us. This is why I refer to these truths as experiences. Moses experienced it. The Apostles experienced it. Also, the early members of the Church experienced it. It is for us to experience.

It amazes me the number times the apostles would speak of the grace of God. The Apostles speak of grace 129 times in the scriptures. The manner in which they would speak of grace is nothing like what we hear today. The body of Christ has reduced grace to an attitude or kind act of God. That is far from the truth. Grace is what God is. Grace is Love's action. Grace is alive in us. You are who you are because of grace. 1Corinthians 15:10

"But by the grace of God, I am what I am: and his grace which was bestowed upon me was not in vain but I labored more abundantly than they all: yet not I, but the grace of God which was with me." (KJV)

God's favor works in your life. God's grace is upon you, and with you. In 2 Corinthians 9:14 we see that it is also in the believer *"And by their prayer for you, which long after you for the exceeding grace of God IN you." (KJV)* Grace influences the emotions. Grace influences the flesh. Grace is God's influence upon and in the heart, which makes you what you are beloved of God! Never let the grace of God becomes a mere attitude. Let it be Love's influence on the whole of man. Confession allows grace to remain what it is Love's influence on and in your life. Confession allows grace to make you conscious of Love's influence in and on your life.

When Paul had prayed three times about a spirit that the enemy had assigned to him to buffet him, he received this revelation:

"And he said unto me, My grace is sufficient for thee: for my strength is made perfect in weakness. Most gladly therefore will I rather glory in my infirmities, that the power of Christ may rest upon me." 2 Corinthians 12:9 (KJV)

Paul realized that the grace of God provided everything he needed to deal with any situation. Paul saw that grace released the power of love in his life. Not only did grace release the power of God but also it caused that power to rest upon him. I bare witness of that in my own life. As you become more conscientious of God's opinion of you, the power of grace will affect your life. Grace, the power of God will abide upon, with and in you. The power of God will increase in your life more than you could even ask or think.

I will always remember the time I became aware that God's power was continually on me. I was having casual conversation with someone afterwards we shook hands. I knew that my hand were very warm. That usually happens when the anointing is upon me. I was not aware when I shook that sister's hand. The power of God flowed into her. She looked at me and said, "Wow, I'm very wobbly. I can barely stand." For me it was strange. I had not preached or taught. Therefore, I did not think the anointing was upon me. Nevertheless, it was as if I had been preaching or teaching. From that, time on my soul was awakened that God's power is continually on me.

While ministering, on other occasions, the love of God was so strong it overwhelmed me. The intensity was so great the Holy Spirit has told me not to touch anyone. He said, blow on them." When I did, they fell to the floor. I watched them try to get up for 15 to 20 minutes. None of them could get up until Grace had finished His perfect work. That is the power of Grace. Through that experience of God's influence upon my life, it embedded love in my consciousness.

You can be conscious of that influence upon your life. As it was given to me, it was given to you. In Ephesians 4:7 (KJV) we see this, ***"But unto every one of us is given grace according to the measure of the gift of Christ."*** What is measure of grace which is the gift of Christ? That measure is abundance of grace.

"And God is able to make all grace abound toward you that ye, always having all sufficiency in all things, may abound to every good work:" 2 Corinthians 9:8 (KJV)

God wants **ALL** grace to abound toward you. That gift of Christ will cause us to **ALWAYS** have sufficiency in everything. That gift of Christ will cause our flesh to abound to every good work. That is a promise to those who love the Lord. *"Grace be with all them that love our Lord Jesus Christ in sincerity. Amen."* Ephesians 6:24 (KJV). Love always remains the root of all God's gifts. Grace will be with you when you sincerely love the Lord. To love the Lord is to keep His commandment to love one another as Christ has loved us.

How precious is the grace of God, which influences the heart, feelings, flesh, and very life. Grace is what the whole person of God exercises towards the believer *"The grace of the Lord Jesus Christ, and the love of God, and the communion of the Holy Ghost, be with you all. Amen."* 2 Corinthians 13:14(KJV). Grace is the influence of the Father, Son, and Holy Ghost. God's grace influences the heart and reveals that you have the love of the Godhead bodily. What an influence grace is, which causes the soul to be love conscious. What an influence it is, that will transform your mind to the mind of Christ.

The Mind of Christ

Earlier in this chapter I discussed confession brings salvation (Rom. 10:10). When you confess the Word, it brings salvation from sickness, oppression, and poverty to healing, deliverance, prosperity. Deliverance/salvation is for all three parts of man, spirit soul and body. It is our soul that needs saving!

"Wherefore, put away all filthiness and overflowing of wickedness, and receive with meekness the engrafted Word, which is able to save your souls." James 1:21 (KJV).

If your soul received, salvation when you became born again than the Holy Spirit would not have inspired that statement. Paul was talking to believers when he said *"And be renewed in the spirit of your mind"* Eph. 4:23(KJV). What is the spirit of your mind? It is your soul. Your soul, which resides in your brain, has two parts: The fleshly part; emotions, senses, intellect, reasoning and spiritual part; your will, personality, character and nature. When you renew the spirit of our mind, a transformation will take place. It will break the process of conforming to this world. God's character and nature will become your character and nature. In Romans 12th chapter, Paul states to present your body unto God, you must renew the mind.

"And be not conformed to this world, but be ye transformed by the renewing of your mind, that ye may prove what is that good, and acceptable, and perfect will of God." Rom. 12:2 (KJV)

Renewing your mind even proves what God's will is. Is this proof for the believer? No, it is for the world to see that you are Jesus' disciples. They will know because you possess God's character and nature in your soul. I like the translation in the Amplified version;

"So get rid of all uncleanness and the rampant outgrowth of wickedness, and in a humble (gentle, modest) spirit receive and welcome the Word which implanted and rooted [in your hearts] contains the power to save your souls."

How do you renew your mind? You renew your mind by receiving the engrafted Word.

How do we receive the engrafted Word? You receive the Word through confessing the Word. That word when confessed will deliver and save your soul. The Word contains the power to save souls. We know this by Romans 1:16

"For I am not ashamed of the gospel of Christ for it is the power of God unto salvation to everyone that believeth to the Jew first, and also the Greek." (KJV)

Some who are reading this and is saying, "I already know about confession." Others will say, "I already know about renewing of the mind." That is good because my purpose is not to teach on confession or renewing of the mind. The Holy Spirit's focus is to get the love of God in your soul and have you act upon it. In order that your mind may become renewed towards God and the world. If you are one that knows about confession and the renewing of your mind, then apply the principles of love. I know that if you apply love to what you already know, it will change your life. To have a renewed mind is to have the mind of Christ. What is the mind of Christ? It is His thoughts, attitudes, pursuits, plans, purposes, and whatever moves His soul. The mind of Christ is the mind of the Father. This is what Paul said Jesus' thoughts were;

"Let this mind be in you, which was also in Christ Jesus: Who, being in the form of God, thought it not robbery to be equal with God: But made himself of no reputation, and took upon him the form of a servant, and was made in the likeness of men: And being found in fashion as a man, he humbled himself, and became obedient unto death, even the death of the cross." Philippians 2:5-8 (KJV)

Though Jesus had striped Himself of all His glory and majesty, He thought it not robbery to make Himself equal with God. The

Word proclaims, let that mind be in you which is in Christ Jesus. You are in the form of God. You are born of Him, created in His image. Not only are you His child but you are one with Him. Jesus was conscious of His oneness with the Father. You must be conscious of the same. You are not taking anything away from God with this consciousness. The Word says so. The problem comes when you don't let this mind be in you. In the body of Christ, our self-concept is so low. We dare to think God would make Himself one with us. We are mere worms, sinners, who God in His greatness was kind enough to save us. We carried this attitude is into the body from when we were in the world's system. We were conforming into the image of the world's system. Renewing the mind throws all the trash of the world out of your mind. You are what God say's that you are and nothing less. To confess anything else is robbery. Any other confession takes the truth and makes it a lie. Our Father is the Father of truth. He said we are beloved of Him and I believe it. I more than believe it. I absolutely know I am beloved of God. You are beloved of God too! The love of God must be in the believer's mind. The commandment that Jesus gave to love one another as He has loved must be the anchor of every believer's souls. Paul said in Romans 7:25

"I thank God through Jesus Christ our Lord. So then with the mind I myself serve the law of God but with the flesh the law of sin." (KJV)

The Word "serve" in the Greek means; to be a slave to be in bondage (do) serve (-ice). Paul said that he had the law of love in his mind. This causes him to be a slave or minister the law of God (love). Paul said with his flesh he could only minister sin.

Romans 8:6-7, tells us:

"For to be carnally minded is death but to be spiritually minded is life and peace. Because the carnal mind is enmity against God: for it is not subject to the law of God, neither indeed can be." (KJV)

When your mind is subject to the law of love, the result is life and peace. It is impossible for the mind that is carnal to be subject to the law of God (love). Confession takes your mind and delivers it from the carnal to the spiritual. All of creation is waiting for all the believers to come to the mind of Christ.

"For the earnest expectation of the creature waiteth for the manifestation of the sons of God. For the creature was made subject to vanity, not willingly, but by reason of him who hath

subjected the same in hope, Because the creature itself also shall be delivered from the bondage of corruption into the glorious liberty of the children of God. For we know that the whole creation groaneth and travaileth in pain together until now." Romans 8:19-22(KJV).

When you possess the mind of Christ, you exercise dominion over the works of God's hands. Hebrews 2:6-8 explains how the believer received dominion. There is nothing that God has not given the believer authority over. Why the body of Christ has not exercised that dominion? The body does not posses the mind of Christ. Most believers do not have love conscious souls. The fullness of that dominion will not be realized until we all come to the same mind as Christ.

"Now I beseech you, brethren, by the name of our Lord Jesus Christ, that ye all speak the same thing, and that there be no divisions among you but that ye be perfectly joined together in the same mind and in the same judgment." 1 Corinthians 1:10 (KJV)

The word "judgment" means; opinion, or resolve (counsel, consent, etc.):—advice, judgment, mind, purpose, will. Paul is speaking to the body of Christ, to speak the same.

When we speak the same, there will be no divisions among the body of Christ. You will know when the body of Christ has come to the mind of Christ. This is because there will be no more denominations. We can join perfectly, in the same mind and purpose. The Holy Spirit would not tell us that we could if we could not. That singleness of mind and purpose comes from love. As a husband and a wife are join in singleness of mind and purpose, so does the body of Christ. It is God's will for the body to have singleness of mind and purpose. The Holy Spirit is instructing all believers to be of singleness of mind in 1 Peter 3:8 ***"Finally, be ye all of one mind, having compassion one of another, love as brethren, be pitiful, be courteous."*** Love is to be on your mind. Compassion one towards another should be your resolve. You will have to set your will to take part of the "consummation of love" in the body of Christ. What is the consummation of love? It is when the whole body of Christ walks in perfect love towards one another. When that consummation takes place it will cause the world to wonder at the love the body demonstrates towards each other. When you walk in perfect love towards the body of Christ, the world will see it. The world will see God, as He really is "love."

In the book of Acts, the love the Church showed for one another was overflowing.

"And all that believed were together, and had all things common, sold their possessions and goods, and parted them to all men, as every man had need. And they, continuing daily with one accord in the temple, and breaking bread from house to house, did eat their meat with gladness and singleness of heart." Acts 2:44-46 (KJV)

They did not want anyone to be lacking in any area when they could supply the need of their brother or sister. Notice there was no mention of a black or white church. There was no mention of a Spanish, Oriental, Korean, Puerto Rican, or ethnic church of any type. It was all the believers together with singleness of heart. Praise God, in the mind of Christ there is no prejudice. There are no color barriers or ethnic barriers in that mind. Oh, how we need that mind that causes all believers to have everything common. The singleness of heart was not a one-time occurrence. It was a way of life for the church. In Acts 4:31-32 illustrates another occurrence:

"And when they had prayed, the place was shaken where they were assembled together and they were all filled with the Holy Ghost, and they spake the Word of God with boldness. And the multitude of hem that believed were of one heart and of one soul: neither said any of them that ought of the

things which he possessed was his own but they had all things common." (KJV)

In Second Chapter of Acts, they had sold everything, and here they sold everything again. Love caused them to prosper. Love consciousness gave them more than they had before they sold their possessions the first time. Also, the power of God shook the building where they were assembled. They were constantly filled with the Holy Spirit. For as you pour out love so is the Holy Spirit pouring out or filling you with love. To see just how important the mind of Christ is to the body of Christ, Hebrews 9:14-15 gives the total picture:

"How much more shall the blood of Christ, who through the eternal Spirit offered himself without spot to God, purge your conscience from dead works to serve the living God? And for this cause he is the mediator of the new testament, that by means of death, for the redemption of the transgressions that were under the first testament, they which are called might receive the promise of eternal inheritance." (KJV)

For what cause is Jesus the mediator of the New Testament? That through the purging of your conscience you might receive the promise of eternal inheritance. It is not an issue of the ability of the blood of Jesus to purge your conscience from dead works. It is up to you to appropriate it or apply it to your soul. Jesus believes it is so important that He is mediating for you to apply it to our soul. I think that says that a purged conscience is very important.

What are the consequences if we do not have the mind of Christ? We cannot receive our eternal inheritance. Jesus loves you too much to see you miss your inheritance. He is constantly trying to work out ways to get you to see that your thoughts must be His thoughts. He is trying to get you to see that His motives must be your motives. He knows that what moves His soul must move your soul. *"What does it profit a man if he gains the world and he lose his soul?"* When you put the love of God in your soul you put God in it (God is Love). God has given us His love. He has given us the mind of Christ. *"For who hath known the mind of the Lord, that he may instruct him? But we have the mind of Christ."* 1 Corinthians 2:16 (KJV) The word "mind" in the Greek means; the intellect, mind (divine or human in thought, feeling, or will) understanding. Praise God, not only will we have His will. Moreover, we will have the understanding of God! Now that is something to get excited about. We will talk more about understanding God in the next chapter. All that is discussed in the last few chapters is captured it this verse;

"Now the end of the commandment is charity (love) out of a pure heart, and of a good conscience, and of faith unfeigned:" 1 Timothy 1:5 (KJV)

The commandment is to love one another as Christ has loved us. The result of that love is a pure heart, a good conscience, and faith unfeigned. That is the mind of Christ. Beloved, that is love consciousness.

A Prayer That God's Opinion Will be Revealed to You

Father, in the name of Jesus, I come to you. Father, I am seeking your face. I desire to know your love. I desire to experience your opinion of me. I have set my will to love the body of Christ. I love you Lord. I pray that manifest your love to me. I believe it is for me to experience in the whole of man spirit, soul, and body. I know the Holy Spirit is inside me, pouring out His love into my heart. I thank you Holy Spirit, for pouring out your love inside me and upon me. For you said Lord that you would manifest yourself. You will manifest yourself to those who have kept your commandments. I will keep your commandments. I know you love me Father. I know you love me Jesus. I know you love me Holy Spirit.

The fire of love is baptizing me. I am filled with your fire. It is consuming me. I know that you are manifesting yourself to me now. Your love is filling me. You are embracing me in your love. Right now, your grace is abounding to me, in me, and with me. I receive the fullness of your love. I receive it in my mind. I receive it in my heart. I receive it in my flesh. I receive it in my spirit. For I am one with you. I am born of love.

I am a love creation. I thank you. Your love is upon me, in me, and with me. I thank you. I will never be the same. This is because;

you manifested your love to me Father. I am your beloved. I thank you that you will continue to demonstrate your love to me until I see you face to face. This is the desire of my heart. In Jesus name. Amen.

Please read this prayer and say the prayer to perceive His love whenever you need to. It is not for a single event or experience. However, the first time will change your life; God will manifest His love time and time again.

If you fall or suppressed with depression, loneliness, or whatever you are going through, God will manifest His love to you in these times. All you have to do is ask and remember this promise;

"And if we know that He hear us, whatever we ask, we know that we have the petitions that we desired of Him." 1 John 5:15(KJV)

My prayer is that this prayer will affect your life as it has affected mine. I desire that you with the whole body will be love conscious. Also, I desire that the fire of love burn in your heart for the entire world, and the body of Christ. I know the Holy Spirit will make Himself more real to you. For this, I thank you Holy Spirit. I love you Holy Spirit. Bless all that read and pray this prayer. Bless them with your love. May the grace of Jesus, and the love of the Father, and the communion of the Holy Spirit be with you. Amen. As you experience God's love and grow in love consciousness God's ways will no longer be unknown to you. The eyes of your understanding will be opened to areas of God's character and nature that where incomprehensible before. God's heart desires that we know Him and understand Him. Understanding God becomes a fact to you for you have the mind of Christ through love consciousness.

Chapter VII

Understanding God Through Love Consciousness

Many times I have heard the phrase; "God's ways are past finding out, for God works in mysterious ways." In reality, I have heard it more times than I cared to. It is sad to think that many people, especially in the church, would believe God is mysterious. Why would go through all that He went through in showing His loving kindness towards us, and remain "mysterious." To believe that is to go against all God has provided in salvation through grace. Those who believe that way are saying love is hidden. Love is never hidden. Love (God) is always manifesting Himself. Why is Love always manifesting Himself? God desires that we know love (Himself) and not have Him hidden from us.

To understand God, you must first come to believe it is for you to understand Him. In 1 John Chapter 4, John tell us, to know love is to know God for God is love. We can agree it is for us to know the love of God, but to know God is another question. It is not another question because the two are the same. The love the Father manifests to us is His essence. He wants all to know His love. He wants you to know Him in His totality.

There is a few verses of scripture (Ephesians 3:16-20) the Lord inspired me several years ago to study and retranslate. He relayed to me there a deeper meaning than appears. In studying, these verses there opened a whole new area in my walk with the Lord. I realized it is more than a prayer. It is the Word of God. The realization came that they were words inspired by the Holy Ghost to edify the whole body of Christ. Those words were Paul's prayer for the church at Ephesus. Before you read, what the Lord had me translate. I would like you to read Ephesians 3:16-20 translation in the King James Version.

"That he would grant you, according to the riches of his glory, to be strengthened with might by his Spirit in the inner man That Christ may dwell in your hearts by faith that ye, being rooted and grounded in love, may be able to comprehend, with all saints, what is the breadth, and length, and the depth, and height, and to knowth love of Christ, which passeth knowledge, that ye might be filled with all the fullness of God."

That is powerful; those verses really open the windows of heaven to us. Let us go a little deeper into what is being said. The verses that you are about to examine have expanded definitions of the Greek words from the original translation. The expanded definitions are there for you to realize the full impact of the word and intent of the writer. The purpose is to know God!

Knowing God

Ephesians 3:16-20

"That He would grant you; according to the fullness of wealth, abundance, and possession (fulfilling them in you) of his glory (very apparent worship, praise, honor, dignity, glory as a result of His good opinion of you), to wax strong, mighty, and to be empowered with miracles, violent strength of wonderful mighty works, power that enables you to do all things by His Spirit dwelling in your inner man (the real you) that Christ may permanently **live** (house) in your thoughts, feelings, and innermost being by the tangibility of your goal—being met and the proof or fact that it can be achieved (faith); that you can be stable, established in love (God's essential Nature and Substance) and to lay hold, eagerly seize, perceive and appropriate with all the saints (Holies of God) what is the width and length, and profoundness of the mystery (the Deep things) and the abundantly (high top) the highest point (of elevation), dignity, and to understand completely, absolutely, and recognize the love of Christ continually, which passes absolute knowledge of spiritual truths, that you would be a miracle worker that is able to perform, anything full, satisfied, crammed, perfect, completely fulfilled with all the substance of God, which fills up the container, the person being filled.

Now unto Him who can do anything, exceedingly, abundantly, above all that we ask, desire, crave, require, think, understand, or exercise our mind by the miraculous power that works in us."

These segments of verses have become my basis in life. It is the culmination of love consciousness in my soul. It is the ability to understand the lover of my soul. It enables me to understand my Father—God, my God—Jesus, my God—Holy Spirit. It is the fulfillment of being as He is in this world.

Look at the first part of the 16th verse "That He would grant you, according to the fullness of wealth, abundance, and possession (fulfilling them in you) of His Glory (very apparent worship, praise, honor, dignity, glory as a result of His good opinion of you)." This is the heart of God concerning you. He desires to fulfill the fullness of wealth, abundance, and His possessions in you. No, that is not materialism. It is what God possesses in Himself. The realization of this next statement is overwhelming. God desires that all His glory that He has fulfilled in you.

The glory God is referring to is the same glory that Moses had on his face. It happened when God reveled Himself to Moses on the cliff of the mountain (Exodus Chapter 34). The same glory fills Heaven and the angelic hosts. The same glory Jesus striped Himself of when

He became sin for us. When Jesus returned to glory, we received that glory with Him. We are His body!

The next portion of that verse says "to wax strong, mighty, and to be empowered with miracles, violent strength of wonderful mighty works, power that enables you to do all things by His Spirit dwelling in your inner man (the real you)." You will wax strong when you know God's opinion of you. When the revelation comes that, He has filled you with His fullness you will know that you are empowered with miracles, violent strength of wonderful mighty works. That strength enables you to do **all** things by His Spirit dwelling in you.

The Holy Spirit will become real to the person who possesses these truths. All things shall be done by the Holy Spirit dwelling inside of you. This is life in the Spirit. Here is love consciousness in those verses "That Christ may permanently live (house) in your thoughts, feelings, and innermost being by the tangibility of your goal—being met and the proof or fact that it will be achieved (faith)." I get excited just thinking about Christ dwelling in my thoughts and feelings. It is a permanent state Jesus living in our thoughts and feelings. Faith is the proof we achieve. Faith is the fact we have what we believe. Not only that but, our faith will make it tangible. I believe this is something full of excitement. Think about

Jesus manifesting Himself in your thoughts and feelings. That is having the mind of Christ.

Where does love come in to all this? Love is the basis of all is spoken in those segments of scriptures. The Holy Spirit continuing said; "That you can be stable, established in love (God's essential Nature and Substance). To lay hold, seize eagerly, perceive, and appropriate with all the saints (Holies of God) what is the width and length, and profoundness of the mystery (the Deep things) and the abundantly (high top) the highest point (of elevation), dignity, and to understand completely, absolutely, and recognize the love of Christ continually." The soul that possesses Christ is the soul that is love conscious. That soul will be stable, established in love. It is the will of God that our souls be stable and established in love. God further desires, that you lay hold, seize eagerly, appropriate, and perceive with all the saints the fullness of that love. You are to perceive the highest point of love, the abundance of love, the dignity of love, the profoundness of love (which has been a mystery), and to LOVE. Love is God's essential character and nature. God desires that you completely understand His love. God expects your understanding of His essential character and nature. What causes you to have that absolute understanding? You have that understanding when you lay hold, seize, appropriate love in your soul.

Therefore, when you retain love consciousness understanding God will be reality. The person in Christ who posses this will not only absolutely understand love. That person will manifest (demonstrate) that understanding of God's character and nature (love). Moreover, the Holy Spirit reveals that you will recognize the love of Christ continually.

Those who possess love consciousness will recognize the love of Christ continually. **We need to recognize the love of Christ surpasses absolute knowledge of spiritual truths.**

You have seen that word absolute several times. To be absolute is to be pure, without anything else. All is impure except whatever is ascertained to be absolute. You have God's pure love, with 100% understanding of that love. The understanding of God's Love surpasses complete understanding of spiritual truths. The understanding of God goes beyond absolute knowledge of spiritual truths. Because, you understand the one who made those spiritual truths. You will know the reason God spoke the words. For you know the spirit in which the writer wrote the words. Isn't that true in the natural? Is it not greater to know the heart of the writer? Is it not greater to know why he choose the words he wrote, than to know the contents only? Sure, it is, and God has given you His heart. He has given you a heart of love. Love inside us revealing everything about

Him. Revealing His thoughts and feelings, His dignity, His praise, His honor, His worship, His profoundness, His power, and all that He is. Know that His totality is in you!

Finally, God said that he who possesses His mind, will be "a miracle worker that can perform, anything fully, satisfied, crammed, perfect, completely fulfilled with all the substance of God, which fills up the container, the one being filled". There is nothing you cannot do when love fills your conscience. You become more than a conqueror. You become satisfied in every good work. Perfection is yours. Full maturity will be a reality to the body of Christ when all believers come to this place together. The reality of God's love packed and overflowing in the body of Christ.

My brothers and my sisters you are complete! Completely fulfilled with all the substance of God-love! This is only a reality to those who possess LOVE CONSCIOUSNESS. Set your will to posses all the substance of God-love. You will never be the same. You will influence lives unlike anything you have seen. You will present God as He really is and people will respond. Expect it, and it will happen in your life as it did in mine.

God will speak to a person that is love conscious what he would not say to a believer that is not love conscious. This is because God knows that the person who is love conscious knows Him. He know what God speaks to him is His character and nature. Furthermore, God knows the person who possesses love consciousness will demonstrate His character and nature. It has become the character and nature of the believer. That is the oneness God expects us to have with Him. This understanding will create unusual circumstances where God will say something to the love conscious soul that is out of the religious norm. The same statement by God to a soul that is not love conscious will not agree with his soul. God's love was not meant for containment in our mental box. Many believers have God in mental boxes and nothing outside of those boxes can be God.

There was a sister in the Lord who was born with a physical defect in her feet. Her feet were curved inwards. When she showed me her feet, they appeared like animal feet. The toes pointed inwards similar to that of a monkey's foot. I describe them this way to give you an image of what I saw. My description is in no way meant to degrade or belittle this dear sister. It took courage for her to show me her feet.

She explained how she had problems (discomfort and pain) with her feet all of her life. God said, "Tell her, I love her. I am going to heal her." God instructed me to tell her to watch her feet. He said,

"For what I am going to do. I want her to see my love for her." I told her all that God had said.

I held her feet in the palm of my hands. As she watched, I closed my eyes and began to pray. When I opened my eyes, I saw that she was crying. I asked her what happened. She told me her feet and toes straightened before her eyes. She further explained it felt as though her toes were pulled straight. As I looked down at her feet, I saw that her feet were normal. The birth defect God completely healed! She also had thyroid problems that I prayed about. I spoke with her a few weeks later. She experienced no problems with her feet from the day we prayed but, her thyroid problems continued.

Why was she healed of one and not the other? She used no faith. What God did, He did because of His love. The purpose of His act of love was to activate her faith for other areas of healing and her life. The same power that straightened her feet was there to take care of the thyroid problem. What God manifested to her showed His commitment to her.

Many who would have ministered under these circumstances would not have prayed with her. They would have waited until they perceived she activated her faith to receive her healing. In addition, various believers would have doubted whether it was the voice of God

Brian Toliver

telling them to pray. They would not believe God would tell them to pray for someone who did not exercise faith or believe for healing. When you understand God it is not a question is it His voice or not. The person who has love consciousness understands God and knows it is God. Not wondering why God said what He said.

That sister will always remember the act of love God demonstrated to her. Similar instances have happened where I ministered to some that had no faith for healing. God healed people who were not believers at all. God is no respecter of persons. He will do the same for one as another. In return, God will expect your faith to arise in love and take Him at His Word.

When you understand God, there are no questions unanswered. Every time you experience God, as I did with that sister. Your awareness of God's character and nature will grow deeper. You know that you know the Father. No, I am not saying you will never learn another aspect about God. You will learn more about Him that will confirm that you know Him. It is the same as a husband and his wife. They know each other but as they exercise their commitment of love to each other, their knowledge of each other grows stronger. It is the same way with God.

110

I will say this about love consciousness that will set some minds at peace. Since I have love consciousness, I am satisfied. I am satisfied like never in my entire life. The hunger to know God, He filled. I still seek Him. No, it is not to know him. I seek him to be with the one my soul loves.

I have told some in the body that I am satisfied. My quest was over to know God. I now can say I understand Him. People have viewed me as if I was crazy. I thought to myself. Do they believe the sermon that Jesus preached on the mountain? ***"Blessed are they that hunger and thirst after righteousness they shall be filled"*** (Matthew 5:6). Jesus made this a promise to those who hunger and thirst. Will you be not only satisfied but also filled! God filled me and you can be to. If, you receive the consciousness of God's love in your soul.

No longer can anyone tell you, you cannot know God. You can say that not only do I know Him but also I understand Him completely. Wouldn't you like to say that? You can say that if you take hold of the love of God in your soul. That is peace. Love's peace will guard your soul. The amplified says in Philippians 4:7

"And God's peace [be yours, that tranquil state of a soul that assured of its salvation through Christ, and so fearing nothing

from God and content with its earthly lot of whatever sort that is, that peace] which transcends all understanding, shall garrison and mount guard over your hearts and minds in Christ Jesus."(KJV)

Love consciousness delivers the soul. It assures you of your soul's salvation. Fear cannot touch you. 2 Timothy 1:7 says *"For God hath not given us the spirit of fear but of power, and of love, and of a sound mind."* *(KJV)* With Love's peace, you will become satisfied. No matter what earthly lot you are in. You will remain sound. God's power (love) becomes your peace. The peace of God will be like a fortress. It will be an army garrison that will mount guard over your heart and mind.

The Holy Spirit will become so special in your life. As He pours that love out into your heart, you will never want Him to leave. Love consciousness will make you so sensitive to the Holy Spirit. You will never want to quench Him for He is the source of your love. He is everything in the believer that is God. The oneness with the Holy Spirit will be a treasure to you. All of this happens because of love consciousness. I am ever grateful to God, for fulfilling His substance in me, through the Holy Spirit by love.

I pray that you can say the same in your life. Because, you mean that much to me! I need you. I need to demonstrate love to you as Christ has. This is purpose of this book.

My desire is be as Christ is towards you. Your desire should be the same. Love compels me to desire this. It consumes me. Receive my love through the words that you have read. When you receive love consciousness in your soul. I know you have received my love. Even greater, receiving love consciousness, you have received the Love of God. God's love is in your soul. Like Paul, Ephesians 3:16—20 has become my prayer for the body of Christ and the world. Allow love to make it your prayer for the world. When this happens, you know you understand love and you know you understand God!

"And we know that the Son of God is come, and hath given us an understanding, that we may know him that is true, and we are in him that is true, even in his Son Jesus Christ. This is the true God, and Eternal Life." 1 John 5:20 (KJV)

Jesus came for all and He gave all an understanding to know Him (referring to the Father). We must demonstrate the understanding we receive through love consciousness. We must demonstrate as Jesus did in His public ministry. The understanding is not only in thought but also in application. The Son of God has given us an understanding how to embody the life of God. Remember, we are in Him. That personification is Eternal Life and proof that God is true. When you exemplify the understanding you have of God, you are imparting Eternal Life and truth.

As you walk in the consciousness of love and the understanding of God those who you share these truths with will see the "True God. "As you have Love's compassion for them, they will see eternal life. The world will learn, through your understanding of God's love, what you apprehended is truth. The purpose of attaining this truth is to pass it to others. For they shall know the truth and the truth shall set them free!

Chapter VIII

The Ministry Of Impartation

Love does not have selfish motives. Love consciousness, Eternal Life and understanding God would mean nothing if you kept it to yourself. As God gave Himself in love so must you. You are one with God through love in Jesus. Therefore, to keep love to yourself or to give love only to those who return your love, is out of God's character. You should desire to give all. That is what a love conscious soul does, gives all. To give all that you are and have is to understand God. Look at what Paul said to the Thessalonians;

"So being affectionately desirous of you, we were willing to have imparted unto you, not the gospel of God only, but also our own souls, because ye were dear unto us." 1 Thessalonians 2:8 (KJV)

Love causes desires that appear crazy to others but real to some because they realize they are dear to you and God. Just imagine being willing to impart your soul to someone because they mean that much to you. Well you mean that much to me. This is what this book is about, imparting my soul unto you. It is not my soul only, but the soul of God that He imparted to you. Imparting is a ministry that is spoken little of or if not at all.

The love you receive you are to impart it to your brothers and sisters in the body of Christ. Love's impartation is necessary for those who do not know God. They will receive the Love of God and it will save their souls. Impartation provides needs were naturally they would not to fulfillment.

Why is impartation a ministry? Its purpose is to establish you. In Romans 1:11(KJV) Paul said *"For I long to see you, that I may impart unto you some spiritual gift, to the end ye may be established."* Impartation is a principle taught through example and precept by Jesus. Jesus said in Luke 3:11(KJV) *"He answereth and saith unto them, He that hath two coats, let him impart to him that hath none and he that hath meat, let him do likewise."* Impartation is not for material needs it is also, for spiritual needs. Everyone needs love. Love is the vehicle impartation uses to give the person in need. Where we fall short, is the impartation of Spiritual gifts.

Impartation of Spiritual Gifts

Impartation takes that which you possess and cause you to make it another's possession. That principle just does not apply to food or clothing it applies to spiritual possessions also. There is an example of this by Peter and John at the gate called Beautiful in Acts 3:6 *"Then Peter said, Silver and gold have I none but such as I have I give thee: In the name of Jesus Christ of Nazareth rise up and walk."* What did Peter possess? Peter possessed healing. He gave healing to him that had need of healing. God desires for us to do the same. When we needed salvation, God imparted salvation unto us through Jesus Christ. All believers are to live by the same principles of impartation.

Impartation is an act of love. Its motivation has purpose and is planned in love. Jesus set the criteria. Jesus said, speaking of the Holy Spirit, in John 16:14 & 16;

"He shall glorify me: for he shall receive of mine, and shall show it unto you. All things that the Father hath are mine: therefore said I, that he shall take of mine, and shall show it unto you." (KJV)

The Holy Spirit will impart all that is the Father's unto you. For what is the Father's is Jesus'. Jesus has imparted all that is the Father's unto you through the Holy Ghost. Jesus further explains in John 17:10 & 22;

"And all mine are thine, and thine are mine and I am glorified in them. And the glory which thou gavest me, I have given them that they may be one, even as we are one."(KJV)

The glory that I referred to in Ephesians 3:16-20, in the previous chapter, is what He is speaking of here. The fullness of wealth, abundance, and possession (fulfilling them in you) of His glory (very apparent worship, praise, honor, dignity, glory as a result of His good opinion of you) is what Jesus has given you. Why has He given you this? He has given you this to confirm you are one with Him, even as He and the Father are one. Jesus imparted the same oneness that He and the Father have, through love. Love gives us the responsibility to do the same. To impart that oneness to those who have not received or experienced it.

Impartation is tangible. You can experience the act of imparting. As it is in natural so, is it in the spiritual. When someone gives, you a gift and you take it in your hands and open it. The emotions that go with receiving it and the joy of getting something you really need said much about the person giving the gift. Those experiences will forever remain in your memory. Each of us still can remember who gave us certain gifts. Because, they were so special to you. Impartation does the same in the spiritual. It is an experience that becomes embedded in your soul.

You are to impart your love consciousness to those who have need of it. Who is it that needs it? The whole body of Christ needs love consciousness imparted unto them. The ministry of impartation will bring the unity to our faith. Our unity of faith will cause us comprehend with all the saint the fullness of His love. The ministry of impartation is love consciousness in action.

I have mentioned before the mind of the early church, towards loving each other. Here, I must refer to it again. In Acts 2:45, the ministry of impartation was a reality.

"And sold their possessions and goods, and parted them to all men, as every man had need."(KJV)

What is the result of love consciousness in action? Acts 4:32 says

"And the multitude of them that believed were of one heart and of one soul: neither said any of them that ought of the things which he possessed was his own but they had all things common." (KJV)

The result was one heart, the heart of God! The result was one soul, the soul of Christ! Everything they received spiritually and physically became common among them. The ministry of impartation is an exercise of love. It flows through your soul as you labor in love. In Ephesians 4:28 (KJV), Paul tells us: *"Let him that stole steal no more: but rather let him labour, working with his hands the thing which is good, that he may have to give to him that needeth."* When you work, you work not only for your own needs but also, for the needs of the body. There is no room for selfishness in a love conscious soul. As a believer, you are to give because you have love towards those who believe.

How should the believers give toward one another in the ministry of impartation? Romans 12:8 calls us to impart our ministry gifts in this manner; *"Or he that exhorteth, on exhortation: he that giveth, let him do it with simplicity he that ruleth, with diligence he that showeth mercy, with cheerfulness."* (KJV) The Amplified Bible translation describes this differently when referring to giving; *"Do it in simplicity and liberality."*

You may think that the ministry instructions have nothing to do with love. Verse 9 & 10 in Romans 12 says:

"Let your love be sincere—a real thing hate what is evil (loathe all ungodliness, turn in horror from wickedness), but hold fast to that which is good. Love one another with brotherly affection—as

members of one family—giving precedence and showing honor to one another." (Amplified Version).

After saying, he who ministers giving or imparting do it with sincerity and liberality, the Holy Spirit said let your love be sincere. Love is understood to be the purpose and motive of your imparting or giving. We should love one another with brotherly affection, as members of one family. That love will give precedence and show honor to one another. That sounds like the statement referring to the believer filled with his glory (remember wealth, dignity, honor, praise, etc.).

God wanted us to we impart, the same way God imparts unto us. He did this because He wanted us to have those experiences. God wanted us to experience what He experiences. Those experiences are the same He does when imparting unto us. God wants us understand not only in word, but also in deed. God wants us to understand why He performs certain actions towards us.

Impartation is experiencing the understanding of God in your flesh. Causing you to know unconditionally, and totally understand God, in your spirit, soul, and body. You fulfill Love's call by demonstrating love towards all in your sphere of influence. The ministry of impartation completes love consciousness in the whole of man. We are born of love (Love of God). When we receive that imparted love in our soul (love consciousness) will live in you. The ministry of impartation will cause Love conscious flow out of your body. Love consciousness cannot be contained. Without expressing that love consciousness, the act of receiving it in our soul would mean nothing. Love without action is dead. I can say that because faith works by love. Therefore, if faith without works is dead, so is love without works is dead.

I exhort you with Jude 1:21

"Guard and keep yourselves in the love of God expect and patiently wait for the mercy of our Lord Jesus Christ, the Messiah, [which will bring you] unto life eternal." (Amplified Version)

Exercising, guarding, and keeping yourself in the love of God will cause the mercy (the active compassion) of God to come to bring you to the life that the Father has Eternal Life. This is the ministry of impartation. We are all called to this ministry. That is the ministry of love.

CHAPTER IX

LOVE IS HOLY

There is an element of love that is taken very lightly. In some cases it is not a consideration at all. All believer and non-believers need to be aware that love is Holy. We need to have that truth in our conscience. I received this revelation in a dream. In the dream I was preaching at a church. While preaching "Love Is Holy" the power of God (love) was greatly demonstrated. It was the first time I received a revelation in this way. I had not received a revelation on scriptures; I was not studying and meditating on. The revelation came very powerful in the dream. The dream was as if I was awake and conscious of what the Lord was saying to me. Afterwards, I did go into an in-depth study on the subject. From that day forward, I never took the love that is God, lightly. I knew love was important. Nevertheless, I had not realized that Love was Holy.

When I had awaken from this dream I rushed to look at the scriptures that I saw myself speak about. Some of the scriptures, which in the natural, I had no knowledge they existed. In the dream, I knew the scriptures that naturally I did not know. As I found each verse of scripture, I awakened to the reality that love is Holy. (I did go on to preach this message at a church. All that God showed me the dream happened the same as the dream.) This scripture tied together all that I had learned of love;

"Wherefore the law is Holy, and the commandment Holy, and just, and good." Romans 7:12 (KJV)

Everything that relates to the law and the commandments are just and good. The Word is Holy. The law is Holy. The commandment is Holy. The law and the commandments are fulfilled in love.

"For all the law is fulfilled in one word, even in this Thou shalt love thy neighbor as thyself." Galatians 5:14(KJV)

Also, stated in Matthew 22:37-40

"Jesus said unto him, Thou shalt love the Lord thy God with all thy heart, and with all thy soul, and with all thy mind. This is the first and great commandment. And the second is like unto it, Thou shalt love thy neighbor as thyself. On these two commandments hang all the law and the prophets."(KJV)

Everything written in the law and of the prophets hang or foundation is love. In the Old Testament, the only way the people of God could see the Holiness of God was through the law. In the New

Testament, we see Holiness through law of love, which fulfills all the law in us.

We read in 1 John 5:2-3 pertaining to love and the commandments;

"By this we know that we love the children of God, when we love God, and keep His commandments. For this is the love of God, that we keep His commandments: and His commandments are not grievous." (KJV)

Keeping the commandments is the love of God. The commandments are Holy; therefore, the keeping of the commandment must be Holy. Keeping the commandments is keeping Holiness. Love brings Holiness into reality. Love consciousness is the placing of Holiness or sanctification in the soul. Holiness in itself is a power that is esteemed and worshiped. Holiness means being full of awe. Holiness, the awe—inspiring presence of God. That is what happened to Moses when he saw God. The Love that is God flooded his soul. It produced Holiness that was visible to the naked eye. It produced the Glory of God on his face. We have a better covenant built on better promises (Heb. 8:6). How much more will the Holiness of God (love) affect our soul? God is love. God is Holy. Love in your soul causes your soul to become Holy as God's Soul is Holy. If, that is not true than we did not receive Love. That would mean. God is not who He said He is.

I believe He gave all of Himself to us. Do you believe He gave all of Himself to you? I saw this began to happen with people who I would meet. The awe and Holiness of God would affect them. Some would begin to reveal what was on their conscience. Sometimes it would make people and family uncomfortable. I would know this because they would come back later and tell me why they felt uncomfortable.

I recall while in Israel. My Rabbi Tour guide pointed me out. He said he knew I was God's child. He said he could see it in my face. This brought me to tears because of all that God had showed me concerning Love and it being Holy.

We are on the cusp of the greatest display of God's Love and Power the earth has ever seen. The Word of God says all of the earth, nature and animals moan and wait for the manifestation of the glory; that will be revealed in the children of God.

"I consider that the sufferings of this present time are not worth comparing with the glory about to be revealed to us. For the creation waits with eager longing for the revealing of the children of God;"
Romans 8:18-19 (NRSV)

Love consciousness in the believer will bring the Holiness/Glory of God to all creation. This is not a wish but it is a promise of God!

You are Holy

Jesus prayed in John 17:17 & 19 (KJV) *"Sanctify them through thy truth: thy Word is truth. And for their sakes I sanctify myself, that they also might be sanctified through the truth."* The Greek word used in the text "sanctify" means to make Holy, purify or consecrate (mentally) to venerate {remember the blood of Jesus purging our conscience in Chapter 7.} You know that Jesus was already Holy and pure. What is He referring to when He said, "I sanctify Myself"? The sanctification He was referring to is the sanctification of His soul. His soul experienced temptation in all points as your soul experiences temptation (Heb. 4:15). As we have established before, the Word is love. Jesus applied (The Word) love to His soul and made His soul Holy.

Jesus fulfilling Holiness in His soul enables you to fulfill it in your soul. Love producing Holiness in your souls is necessary for your presentation unto the Lord as Holy. In Ephesians 5:25-27, we see Jesus' attitude towards the church and sanctification.

"Husbands, love your wives, even as Christ also loved the Church, and gave Himself for it that, He might sanctify and cleanse it with the washing of water by the Word, That he might present it to Himself a Glorious Church, not having spot, or

wrinkle, or any such thing but that it should be Holy and without blemish."(KJV)

These verses of scripture sound like John 17: 17 & 19 that you earlier read, but go a little further. Jesus wants the Church to be Holy! Jesus wants a Glorious Church! Do you think He will have a Glorious Church? Do you think He will have a Holy Church? Unequivocally, yes He will have a Glorious and Holy Church. This is because God has given us His love and that Love that is inside us makes us Glorious and Holy.

We are responsible for presenting ourselves Holy (not making ourselves Holy) to the Lord. Remember Romans 12:1 *"I beseech you therefore, brethren, by the mercies of God, that ye present your bodies a living sacrifices, Holy, acceptable unto God, which is your reasonable service."* How do you present yourself Holy? The next verse tells you. It is by renewing your soul. Without the soul having love consciousness, your flesh could not be presented Holy unto God. When your soul is in line with your spirit, your flesh will have to follow. The most of the body of Christ has not put their spirit, soul in authority over their flesh. We are exhorted in 1Thessalonians 4:4 *"That every one of you should know how to possess his vessel in sanctification and honour."(KJV)* This is what this book is all about—**how to possess God in your spirit, soul, and body through love.**

Paul through the Holy Spirit said in 1 Thessalonians 5:23

"And the very God of peace sanctify you wholly and I pray God your whole spirit and soul and body be preserved blameless unto the coming of our Lord Jesus Christ." (KJV)

God will make you Holy wholly—spirit, soul, and body when love takes over your consciousness. It is up to you if you retain love consciousness or not. The Holy Spirit is pouring out Holy love in your hearts to make you like your Holy Father. As you take the truths; that you are born of love and your faith is of love. Then you confess the Word (that is love) it will renew your soul through love consciousness and you understand God. With your understanding of God and love consciousness, it will be imparted to others. Love will make Holiness visible in your life. The process of sanctification will be complete in your life through love consciousness.

"But He that has called you is Holy, so be Holy in all manner of conversation (life), because it is written, Be ye Holy for I am Holy." 1 Peter 1:15-16 (KJV)

If your desire is to see God, than be Holy as He is Holy for without Holiness no man shall see God (Hebrews 12:14). You will never see God's fullness in this life or that, which is to come without the Holiness that love consciousness provides. 1 Peter 1:22, summarizes this chapter perfectly, but I will amplify some words to insure realization of the full meaning.

"Seeing that ye have purified (sanctified, made Holy, consecrated and venerated) your souls in obeying the truth through the (Holy) Spirit unto unfeigned loved of the brethren, see that ye love one another with a pure (Holy, sanctified) heart fervently."

That is the power love! The power of love makes your soul Holy through obedience to the Holy Spirit. The Holy Spirit pours the love of God (God is Love) into your heart. The power of love sanctifies your heart when you show love towards God's people. You become Holy as God is Holy when your love is burning with compassion towards God's people. This Holy love is the victory, which overcomes the world! We have an invitation to this glorious victory through the power of love in Holiness. None that is unholy will stand against you. Because, you are Holy through love. That Holiness in your soul will bring God's Glory in your life and affect your soul as it did Moses. You have the fullness of God (Holiness, wealth and abundance of His Glory) fulfilling them in you!

CHAPTER X

LOVE'S CALL TO GLORY

Something the Holy Spirit has revealed to me that love will bring us to the fullness of God. I mentioned this in certain portions of this book. When you have a small concept of God, it is incomprehensible to conceive in your mind the fullness of God. God's Spirit compelled me to describe some of the points He has revealed. These points are concerning God's fullness as it pertains to the body of Christ.

As I have mentioned before it is God's will that He would grant you, according to the fullness of wealth, abundance, and possession (fulfilling them in you) of His Glory (very apparent worship, praise, honor, dignity, Glory as a result of His good opinion of you)[Eph. 3:16]. God wants us full of His Glory. He desires to fulfill His Glory in you. This is a promise to those who possess and comprehend the fullness of His love [Eph. 3:16-20.] This promise is a call to glory. This is seen in 1 Peter 5:10

"But the God of all grace, who hath called us unto His Eternal Glory by Christ Jesus, after that ye have suffered a while, make you perfect, stablish, strengthen, settle you."(KJV)

You will suffer because of love. That suffering is the rejection from others of love you give. It is the most difficult part of giving love. This is the cross of Jesus that we must bear. Our cross to bear is the rejection of perfect love and not sickness and disease. I struggled for a long time with rejection. Sometimes, I would feel like never allowing myself to be vulnerable to rejection. The pain would be unbearable at times. This rejection continued, until I knew I could go to the Father. In addition, I realized the rejection was not towards me. The rejection is really that person rejecting God's Love. I learned that He would manifest His love towards me to strengthen me and settle my heart.

Praying about rejection was good. Regardless, it is not the same as knowing and receiving God's Love. I would receive God's Love tangibly in the flesh and upon my soul. Receiving God's Love upon the flesh, and soul, satisfies any soul. God's Love bestowed upon you strengthens your inner man. The strengthening occurs through God's Spirit. God's Spirit pours love into you and upon you. This is when God's Glory comes. Why does God's Glory come? It comes because of the sanctification of your heart. Each time you choose to love your heart becomes pure, perfect, Holy (sanctified) through love. As rejection comes, you begin to understand and experience the fellowship of His suffering. This is the process of God's Glory filling your life. Not all will reject, as not all will receive. The conclusion that I have come to, is whatever rejection I experience, it is worth it. It is worth it if just one comes to know the love of God. You may say, "Who wants rejection?" No one wants rejection. Keep in mind, Love is not selfish. Love does not seek its own. When you can say, "Rejection means nothing in my life. All that matters is manifesting the love of God." Then, you have mortified the deeds of the flesh. My brother and sister, that is moving on to perfection (Holiness).

Holiness produces the Eternal Glory of God. There is no manifestation of God's Glory in the lives of believers. Why? Love has not finished its perfect work in their heart. How does Love finish it's perfect work? It is through Patience. James reveals this in the Scriptures.

"My brethren, count it all joy when you fall into various trials, knowing that the testing of your faith produces patience. But let patience have its perfect work, that you may be perfect and complete, lacking nothing." James 1: 2-4(NKJV)

We established faith works by love. When rejection tests your faith (motivated by love), it produces patience. Patience produces a perfect work that makes you perfect and complete and lacking nothing. You can count it all joy when you are complete and lacking nothing!

Another reason there is no manifestation of God's Glory in the lives of believers. The reason is they don't believe it is for them to receive God's Glory. Tradition causes the few that have perfected hearts not to believe it is for them to receive God's visible Glory. In many churches, the expectation that the Glory of God will roll in the building like a cloud is viable. When it comes to believing we can have the Glory of God manifested upon our flesh, we say never. Do you believe God counts a building more worthy to receive His Glory than His children? Moses did not think that way. He asked God to show him his Glory.

We see this In **Exodus 33; 18-23 (KJV)** *"And he said, "Please, show me Your glory." Then He said, "I will make all My goodness pass before you, and I will proclaim the name of the LORD before you. I will be gracious to whom I will be gracious, and I will have compassion on whom I will have compassion." But He said, "You cannot see My face; for no man shall see Me, and live." And the LORD said, "Here is a place by Me, and you shall stand on the rock. So it shall be, while My glory passes by, that I will put you in the cleft of the rock, and will cover you with My hand while I pass by. Then I will take away My hand, and you shall see My back; but*

My face shall not be seen." God did what Moses asked. Surprisingly, when Moses came down from the mountain he was different. Exodus 34:29-30 (KJV) *"Now it was so, when Moses came down from Mount Sinai (and the two tablets of the Testimony were in Moses' hand when he came down from the mountain), that Moses did not know that the skin of his face shone while he talked with Him." So when Aaron and all the children of Israel saw Moses, behold, the skin of his face shone, and they were afraid to come near him.* Moses had God's physical Glory radiating from his face. Moses had to place a veil over is face to cover God's visible Glory. Exodus 34:32-33 (KJV) *"Afterward all the children of Israel came near, and he gave them as commandments all that the LORD had spoken with him on Mount Sinai. And when Moses had finished speaking with them, he put a veil on his face."* When God reveals his Glory to you, it will be visible to all around you. Moses is a great example of what happens when God reveals His "Goodness." Moses shows us the results of God's character and nature revealed to man's soul.

Over the years, the body of believers learned through teachings God will not share His Glory with anyone. In addition, anyone who receives glory that is due to God, He will abase. God will share His Glory. He said so. Not only did He say He would give us His Glory but He will fulfill His Glory is us. Yes, God will abase those receiving glory due to Him. There is a great difference from taking glory that is God's and receiving Glory from God. One is an act of rebellion the other is an act of love.

We do not deserve this act of love. It is a gift. This is what Grace is all about. God thinks this much about you that He would fill you with His Glory. Moreover, you are not the same person you were before you became a believer. Again, it is no longer you it is God inside you. The two of you have become one. He sees no difference in you and Him. Meditate on this thought. If, God cannot fully dwell in you than God cannot live in you. God stated He would live in the believer. Is His Glory apart of Him? Yes, the Glory is a part of God. It is an important part that He desires to fulfill in the body of Christ.

Once again look at Moses; He physically manifested the Glory of God permanently. Why, didn't Jesus manifest the Glory permanently? That is because He striped Himself of all Glory. Even at that, He still manifested it at different times. I ask you this. Is Moses greater than Jesus that He should walk in the Glory of God and Jesus did not? In Hebrews 3:1-3, Paul speaks of this;

*"**Wherefore, Holy brethren, partakers of the heavenly calling, consider the Apostle and High Priest of our profession, Christ Jesus Who was faithful to him that appointed him, as also Moses was***

faithful in all his house. For this man was counted worthy of more glory than Moses, inasmuch as he who hath builded the house hath more honour than the house."(KJV)

Jesus had more glory than Moses did. For He, Who built the house has more honour than the house. The scriptures speak much about the house. One prophesy in Haggai 2:7 (KJV) says *"And I will shake all nations, and the desire of all nations shall come: and I will fill this house with glory, saith the LORD of hosts."* You are the house that God wants filled with His glory. In verse 9 (KJV), Haggai further proclaims through the Holy Spirit *"The glory of this latter house shall be greater than of the former, saith the LORD of hosts: and in this place will I give peace, saith the LORD of hosts."* Moses house was the former house and our house (the house of Christ) is the latter. The Lord said that the latter will be greater than Moses house. Joel 2:23 says;

"Be glad then, ye children of Zion, and rejoice in the LORD *your God: for he hath given you the former rain moderately, and he will cause to come down for you the rain, the former rain, and the latter rain in the first month."(KJV)*

The former rain came moderately. The latter rain will come down! We should be glad that we are chosen to house the Glory of

God in the earth. Adam and Eve initially wore the Glory of God as clothing, in Genesis 2:25. Jesus gave us back that glory. Remember Chapter 8.

No longer is the Glory of God confined to a tent or the Holy of Holies, but shall fill living temples not made of hands. In Zechariah 10:1 we are told, *"Ask ye of the LORD rain in the time of the latter rain so the LORD shall make bright clouds, and give them showers of rain, to every one grass in the field."* We are to ask the Lord to rain in the time of the latter rain. This is the time of the latter rain. These are the last days. God said He would make bright clouds. Those clouds are the glory of Love upon our spirit, soul, and body. He promised to give the clouds showers of rain.

Beloved, God desires that His fullness of Glory become fulfilled in us. It is more than a desire it is a promise. God's Glory becomes fulfilled in us when, His love becomes fulfilled in us. I have seen it in the spirit.

I say this by the Holy Spirit. There is a day coming, that God's Glory will physically be seen on our flesh. Remember (Ephesians 3:16) in Chapter 7, the first part of the 16th verse said "That **He would grant you**, according to **the fullness of wealth, abundance, and possession (fulfilling them in you) of His Glory**

(very apparent worship, praise, honor, dignity, glory as a result of His good opinion of you)." God will grant the Body of Christ His Glory. The Glory, He occupies is the same Glory, He will grant us. The nations will know we are of God. Some people will run to us and others will run away. All that is wicked will hate the very thought of our presence. The Wicked will do anything to prevent us from walking around in the Glory of God. Remember, we have a better covenant than Moses did and he had God's Glory. How much more of God's Glory will we have with our covenant built on better promises?

The Glory will Usher in the Return of Christ

God not only spoke to my heart concerning His Glory. God showed me what He spoke to my heart by a vision. The glory I saw will usher in the return of Christ. For when the fullness of God's Glory is upon us, we will be a twinkling of an eye away from the translation from this world to the next. Those who live the life of love will love His appearing. Jesus is coming for those who love His appearing. Jesus came because of love and love will cause Him to return. 2 Timothy 4:8 states:

"Henceforth there is laid up for me a crown of *righteousness, which the Lord, the righteous judge, shall give me at that day: and not to me only, but unto all them also that love his appearing."(KJV)*

My beloved brothers and sisters what I have seen words cannot describe. How I long for that day to be a reality. How I long for that day, the body of Christ manifests that we are the Sons of God. It is not only my desire. Also, it is creations desire. It is my desire because; the Holy Spirit has caused it to be so. It is my desire because, of a **Love Conscious soul. Love Consciousness** will make it your desire too!

CONCLUSION

Some may try to say that this book places focus on the experience and not the Word. That is far from the truth. We get our experiences through the Word of God. Those experiences make the Word come alive (real) to us. When the Holy Spirit spoke to me concerning writing this book, the purpose was to reveal and bring all believers together in love. I pray that love has awakened you. I pray that the Holy Spirit will make the words of this book a reality in your life as He did mine. I trust that He will. All that I wrote in this book was His will.

I have seen God confirm the words in this book repeatedly. God has confirmed these words in all types of lives. The results are still the same—a changed life. A life touched by love (God) in a very personal way. The way that says, "I have a good opinion of you (grace)." Nothing can separate us from the love of God. Love is the proof of this truth. Let God the Father, Son, and Holy Spirit manifest themselves (Love) to you. You will experience a satisfaction that you never experienced before. You will become filled with the fullness of God. All of this is because you allowed your soul to possess Love Consciousness.